AVIATION AND AIRPORT SECURITY

MANAGEMENT, IMPROVEMENT STRATEGIES AND FUTURE CHALLENGES

TRANSPORTATION ISSUES, POLICIES AND R&D

Additional books in this series can be found on Nova's website
under the Series tab.

Additional e-books in this series can be found on Nova's website
under the eBook tab.

AVIATION AND AIRPORT SECURITY

MANAGEMENT, IMPROVEMENT STRATEGIES AND FUTURE CHALLENGES

DON LAWRENCE
EDITOR

nova
science publishers
New York

NOTICE TO THE READER

Library of Congress Cataloging-in-Publication Data

ISBN: 978-1-53611-909-1

Published by Nova Science Publishers, Inc. † New York

CONTENTS

PREFACE

Chapter One summarizes research on the seismic performance of air traffic control (ATC) towers, discusses their shortcomings and puts forward recommendations for future studies. Chapter Two covers the construction of an airport for the capital of Germany that has an erratic history dating back to the early nineties. During the long planning period, the employment impacts of a major airport played an important role in the public dialogue. This chapter sets out how a scenario technique was used to calculate employment effects related to this major airport project. Chapter Three analyzes airport security in the Czech Republic regarding the Safety Risk Management (SRM) setting including the Safety Risk Assessment (SRA) with respect to economic aspects of the issue. The chapter also includes statistical backstage pointing to the topicality of this issue. Chapter Four uses the case of Atlanta Hartsfield/ Jackson International Airport (ATL) to illustrate the links between airport capacity management and passenger satisfaction measured as airlines' on-time performance. Chapter Five covers the potential benefits from using Linked Data technologies in emergency scenarios and presents the authors' applications for improved emergency response.

Chapter 1 - Soon after destructive earthquakes, airports face a rapid increase in the transposition of disaster-related commodities. Dealing with such a rapid increase in demands is possible if vital structures inside airports are functional after ground motions. Air traffic control (ATC) towers are among such vital structures that monitor taking off and landing of airplanes. Unlike common buildings, ATC towers show a complicated dynamic response when they are subjected to earthquakes. So far, seismic design codes have paid less attention to these structures and no specific seismic design guidelines have been published for them. Lack of particular code or design guidelines for ATC towers may lead design engineers to the misuse of seismic codes that are prepared for buildings and bridges. This in return can jeopardize the safety of ATC towers against seismic actions. Despite the lack of specific seismic design guidelines for ATC towers, some researchers have investigated their seismic response and vulnerability. The main aim of this chapter is to summarize the conducted researches on the seismic performance of ATC towers, discuss their shortcomings and put forward recommendations for future studies.

Chapter 2 - The construction of a new single airport for the capital of Germany has an erratic history that dates back to the early nineties. After several postponements in putting the airport into operation, its opening is now projected for the course of the year 2018. During the long planning period the employment impacts of a major airport played an important role in the public dialogue. This paper sets out how a scenario technique was used to calculate employment effects related to this major airport project.

The first assessment approach was utilized to examine alternative sites for the new single airport in the early planning stage. It found that the location of Schönefeld, the site which was finally chosen, would generate the highest effects on employment among the three alternative proposals of suitable sites. The reasons were its short distance to the metropolis of Berlin and its greatest stimulating effects on economic growth in the surrounding area.

The second assessment approach was performed three years before in 2008, prior to the expected opening date of the airport. The mission was to identify industries, occupations and regions in Berlin and Brandenburg that would benefit from air transport services. Based on this information, qualification measures should be developed. In contrast to the usual quantification framework of magnitudes the assessment concentrated on structural changes in employment. The procedure is based on the employment statistics that contains 336 occupations and which is able to map the regional development of air transport related employment in 402 German districts. The employment figures are differentiated according to jobs that are directly located at the airport site, indirect employment effects in the aerospace industry and in related sectors and catalytic effects on the economy as a whole.

The results give evidence for direct and indirect employment effects outside the airport site in Berlin, and for regional effects in the southern districts of Berlin, notably in the counties of Dahme-Spreewald, Teltow-Fläming and Potsdam. It was predicted that aircraft-related industries located in the administrative district of Dahme-Spreewald stimulate the job creation in technical occupations in Brandenburg. The most tentative forecast is related to occupations that benefit from better airport infrastructure via catalytic effects. Those impacts especially were found for service occupations with university degrees such as consultants and managers which are located in Berlin and in the metropolitan areas in Brandenburg.

Chapter 3 - The aviation transport has gone through dynamic development during last years. The airport security also relates to this turbulence in the aviation industry. The large area with huge accumulation of people at the airports and their surroundings has been the reasons for a targeting to an airport security. This chapter deals with the issue of an airport security in the Czech Republic. The Czech Republic has been an important strategic transport node also with its geographical position such as EU and NATO membership. Within the framework of this chapter, the airport security in the Czech Republic will be analyzed regarding the Safety Risk Management (SRM) setting including the Safety Risk Assessment (SRA) with respect to economic aspects of the issue. The chapter also includes statistical backstage pointing to the topicality of this issue.

Chapter 4 - This study used the case of ATL to illustrate the links between airport capacity management and passenger satisfaction measured as airlines' on-time performance. The analysis relied on several assumptions. First, airport operators and air traffic control play a significant role in minimizing variations in airport capacity utilization, which may affect airlines' on-time performance and, as a result, passenger satisfaction. Reducing process variability and improving gate-to-gate processes both represent the key principles of a lean sigma approach to flight operations. Second, the implementation of NextGen capabilities and procedures reduced the variability of unutilized airport capacity. A comparison of two samples revealed that the standard deviation of unutilized airport capacity decreased, while the sigma level improved from 2.6 (March to May 2015) to 2.9 (March to May 2016) during the core hours of 7:00 to 21:59 (local time). By minimizing the variability of unutilized capacity, airlines reduced gate departures and arrival delays by about two minutes on average compared with airlines' flight plan estimates, while the number of operations and available capacity both increased.

Chapter 5 - One of the most critical aspects of emergency management (EM) is the notification system concerning how to get updated and accurate information from the very first stages of the event and how to notify affected people. The citizens, as the simplest level of participation in an emergency scenario, can act as information consumers (e.g., about alarms, affected areas, instructions for handling critical situation) but also as evidence producers (e.g., via phone or social network).

With the aim to develop a deeper understanding of potential benefits from using Linked Data technologies in emergency scenarios, in this chapter the authors present their current work on building citizen applications for improved emergency response. The paper introduces first the potential areas of applicability of Linked Data in innovative EM solutions and points to early prototypes in Europe based on crowdsourcing, social networks, mobile devices, and open data. Next, software requirements and information flow are analysed for a data ecosystem that facilitates the engagement of citizens leveraging novel approaches such as the participatory sensing approach (knowledge from the wisdom of crowds) and cloud-enabled solutions.

To demonstrate the feasibility of the approach, a prototype application, TraffAccs, has been developed using state-of-the-art open-source tools and frameworks: the Massachusetts Institute of Technology (MIT) Panya framework for implementing the mobile client and Dydra graph database for storing notification messages.

In: Aviation and Airport Security
Editor: Don Lawrence

ISBN: 978-1-53611-909-1
© 2017 Nova Science Publishers, Inc.

Chapter 1

SEISMIC VULNERABILITY OF AIR TRAFFIC CONTROL TOWERS

Mohammadreza Vafaei[1,] and Sophia C. Alih[2]*

[1]Centre for Forensic Engieeirng, Faculty of Civil Engieering,
Universiti Teknologi Malaysia, Johor, Malaysia
[2]Inistitute of Noise and Vibration, Faculty of Civil Engieering,
Universiti Teknologi Malaysia, Johor, Malaysia

ABSTRACT

Soon after destructive earthquakes, airports face a rapid increase in the transposition of disaster-related commodities. Dealing with such a rapid increase in demands is possible if vital structures inside airports are functional after ground motions. Air traffic control (ATC) towers are among such vital structures that monitor taking off and landing of airplanes. Unlike common buildings, ATC towers show a complicated dynamic response when they are subjected to earthquakes. So far, seismic design codes have paid less attention to these structures and no specific seismic design guidelines have been published for them. Lack of particular code or design guidelines for ATC towers may lead design engineers to the misuse of seismic codes that are prepared for buildings and bridges. This in return can jeopardize the safety of ATC towers against seismic actions. Despite the lack of specific seismic design

* Corresponding Author Address: Faculty of Civil Engineering, Universiti Teknologi Malaysia, 81310, Johor, Malaysia; Email:vafaei@utm.my.

guidelines for ATC towers, some researchers have investigated their seismic response and vulnerability. The main aim of this chapter is to summarize the conducted researches on the seismic performance of ATC towers, discuss their shortcomings and put forward recommendations for future studies.

Keywords: air traffic control tower, seismic vulnerability, seismic codes, pushover analysis, nonlinear time history analysis

INTRODUCTION

Air Traffic Control (ATC) towers are employed to regulate arrival, departure and surface movements of aircraft in airports. Historically, the first usage of ATC towers was in 1920 at Croydon Airport, London [1]. By increase in the number of aircraft worldwide, especially after World War II, many airports employed the radio-equipped ATC towers. Nowadays, almost all airports take advantage of ATC towers to prevent collision and facilitate the flow of air traffic.

Although architecturally ATC towers come with different designs, in order to fulfill their duties they are consist of specific components. The first component of ATC towers is the control cab. As can be seen from Figure 1, at the top, where the best unobstructed view is provided for air traffic controllers, the control cab is located. The size of control cab depends on the level of airport activity and the number of operating personnel in the ATC tower. The minimum required surface of the control cab varies from 20 m² for less than 6 personnel to 50 m² for more than 12 personnel [2, 3]. In order to avoid an obstructed view, the control cab is often constructed by a steel structure so that the required sizes for beams and columns are reduced to a minimum. It is worth mentioning that, the perimeter of control cabs is often fully covered by inclined glasses. This fragile coverage makes control cabs a vulnerable structure against extreme loads like strong winds and earthquakes. Below the control cab, the second component of ATC towers is located. As shown in Figure 1, the junction levels provide enough space for mechanical, electrical and elevator equipment together with lavatories. The sizes and numbers of junction levels depend on the activity level and size of the control cab. The third component of ATC towers is the tower shaft. While the main job of this shaft is to provide the required height for the tower, it encompasses the elevators and stairways for accessing to upper floors. The height of the tower shaft is determined by the height of the operating level in such a way that the optimum visual surveillance is obtained. Studies show that the total height of majority of existing ATC towers ranges from 30 m to 100 m with the average height of around 70 m [4]. Structurally, the tower shaft provides the required lateral stiffness against the wind and seismic actions. In addition, it transfers the gravity loads from the control cab and junction levels to foundations. In many tall ATC towers, because of their higher lateral stiffness, concrete walls have been employed as the main lateral load resisting system. In some cases, the combination of steel frames and concrete walls have been used. There are also few short towers that only take advantage of concrete and steel moment resisting frames or braced frames to provide lateral strength and stiffness. The last component of ATC towers is the base building where training, conference and telecommunication rooms together with radar and communication equipment rooms are located. The base building can be included inside the ATC towers or can be constructed as a separate building. Majority of existing ATC towers have a separate base building. This is because often not enough free space can be provided for the base building inside ATC towers.

Figure 1. Air traffic control tower and technical block of Persian Gulf International Airport, Bushehr, Iran.

During past decades the number of constructed ATC towers has had an exponential increase. This has been mainly due to the increase in the number of airports and aircraft worldwide. Forecasting has also shown that the demand for the construction of new ATC towers will increase in the future [4]. This rapid increase in the number of ATC towers should come with a satisfactory safety margin against factors that affect their operation. One of the significant factors that should be taken into account is the vulnerability of ATC towers against earthquakes. Although in literature many descriptive guidelines can be found for the architectural design of ATC towers, the design of ATC towers against extreme loads like earthquakes has not been well addressed. In addition, because of a limited number of ATC tower worldwide, our understanding regarding the seismic performance of ATC towers during past earthquakes is not as much as common buildings. This paper is intended to put together the conducted research on the seismic vulnerability of ATC towers and put forward recommendations for future studies.

SEISMIC PERFORMANCE OF ATC TOWERS DURING PAST EARTHQUAKES

Earthquakes release a significant amount of energy in a short period of time. This in return can shake constructed structures strongly and impose significant damage to them. Existing seismic design codes partially have been built based on our observations from the seismic performance of structures during earthquakes. Therefore, seismic design codes are being improved and updated as new observations and findings are presented by researchers. This clearly demonstrates the significant role of such observations in the vulnerability assessment of ATC towers against earthquakes.

A review of the literature shows that there are only a few cases where seismic induced damages have been reported for ATC towers. This, however, does not mean that these towers have had a good performance against seismic actions in the past earthquakes. One main reason for the few reports on the damaged ATC towers is that unlike common buildings the number of ATC towers are limited in each country. In addition, not all ATC towers have been constructed in the areas with high seismic activity. In spite of such small population, the reconnaissance investigations have demonstrated that ATC towers could be vulnerable against seismic actions even when the intensity of ground motions have not been very strong. One example of seismic induced damage to a newly constructed ATC tower can be found in Qeshm International Airport, Iran. The section of this tower is shown in Figure 2a. The total height of the tower is 34.4 m and as can be seen from this figure it has two junction levels under the control cab. The control cab covers an area with the radius of 6 m while the first and second junction levels have the area of 8x8 m^2 and 15x15 m^2, respectively. The shaft of the tower consists of 4 large columns with the same size of 3.4 m x 0.75 m together with a concrete wall around the lift of tower. Few concrete columns that are distributed in their perimeter and inside, support the junction levels. The roof of control cab is constructed by a concrete slab which is supported by steel trusses. This roof rests on four steel columns that are connected at their base to the roof beams of the junction level (see Figure 3).

The tower was hit by a ML 5.6 earthquake on 27 November 2005 prior to its inauguration. The epicenter of the earthquake was less than 10 km away from the tower. As can be seen from Figures 2b, the control cab of the tower was completely destroyed by the earthquake. Further investigations indicated that the failure of the control cab has been initiated from columns' baseplates. As can be seen from Figure 3b, the base plates of the columns have been connected to the floor through four bolts. However, seismic demands at the base of columns have been much larger than the capacity provided by the bolts. Further investigation showed that, although poor detailing contributed to the failure of the bolts, higher mode shapes' effect significantly increased the seismic demand at the base of the steel columns. The main reason for significant contribution of higher mode shapes was the large difference between the lateral stiffness of the control cab and the shaft of the tower. As mentioned earlier, often the size and the number of columns in the control cabs are reduced to a minimum in order to avoid an obstructed view. Moreover, the perimeter of control cabs is always covered with glass which has a negligible lateral stiffness. Therefore, the lateral stiffness of the control cab often falls significantly below the stiffness of stories below it. This in return shakes the structure of control cab individually in higher modes and imposes large seismic demand to the structural elements of control cab. Figure 4a displays the fourth mode shape of the finite element model of the new ATC tower which is going to replace the old one in Qeshm International Airport (QIA). It is evident from the fourth mode shape that, the control cab is vibrating in the opposite direction of the tower shaft. It is worth mentioning that, the concentration of damage in the softer story (i.e., control cab) is not limited to the ATC tower. Figure 4b displays a damaged Menara belonging to a mosque in Ranau, Malaysia, after 5th June 2015 earthquake with the intensity of

Mw=6. Similar to the ATC tower of QIA the lateral stiffness of the top structure was significantly lower than that of levels below. This has imposed significant damage to supporting columns at the top of this Menara. It should be also mentioned that, although the control cab of the Qeshm International airport was destructed by the earthquake, no significant damage was observed for other structural components. During visual inspections only a few cracks at the beam to column joints were observed.

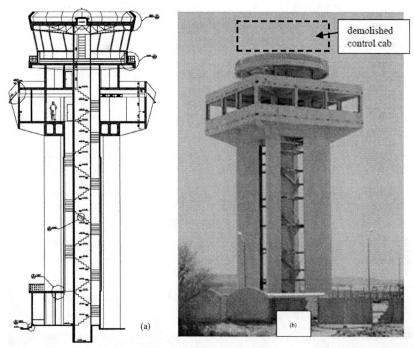

Figure 2. Qeshm Air Traffic Control Tower. (a) Section of the tower (b) Tower after being excited by earthquake.

Reconnaissance reports from other airports also show that the control cab has been the most vulnerable part of ATC towers during past earthquakes. As shown in Figure 5, the windows of the control cab of ATC tower in Seattle–Tacoma International Airport, USA, has been broken after Nisqually earthquake in 28 Feb. 2001. It is noteworthy that even damage to non-structural components can disturb the operation of ATC towers after earthquakes. These observations indicate that in the design of ATC towers against seismic actions especial attention should be given to the seismic demand at the control cab and sensitive non-structural components that are used in that place. A well designed ATC tower not only should be able to limit seismic induced damages to structural elements but also should avoid damage to non-structural components of control cabs.

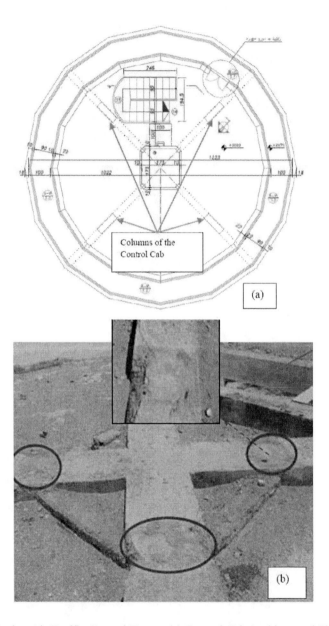

Figure 3. Qeshm Air Traffic Control Tower. (a) Control Cab Architectural Plan (b) Tower after being excited by earthquake.

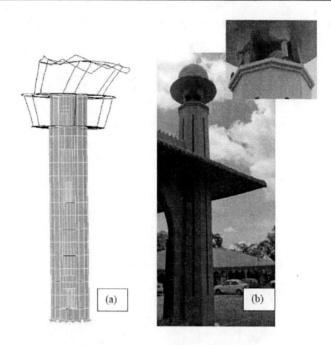

Figure 4. (a) The fourth mode shape of new ATC tower of Qeshm International Airport. (b) Seismic induced damage to a Menara in Sabah, Malaysia.

Figure 5. ATC tower of Seattle–Tacoma International Airport after Nisqually earthquake [5].

SEISMIC VULNERABILITY STUDIES OF ATC TOWERS DURING PAST YEARS

The majority of conducted seismic vulnerability studies have focused on case studies. Although the obtained results from each case study can enhance our understanding regarding the seismic behavior of ATC towers, they may not be valid for other ATC towers. It is noteworthy that, from the architectural point of view, ATC towers are considered as a symbol for airports, therefore, their architectural plan and shape are significantly different from each other. This makes the study on ATC towers more challenging because different architectural shape and plan require different structural system. In one of such case studies, Eshghi and Farrokhi [6] investigated seismic vulnerability of a 62 m tall ATC tower in Imam-Khomeini International Airport, Tehran, Iran. For resisting against lateral loads, the tower took advantage of 4 box-shaped wings around its perimeter. The wings were connected to each other through a reinforced concrete slab with the thickness of 25 cm at 12 levels along the height of the tower. The thickness of the box-shaped wings was constant all along the height and equal to 30 cm. Figure 6 displays the schematic view of the plan and elevation of the tower. Authors established the Finite Element (FE) model of the tower in ANSYS [7] software considering fixed supports at its base. From the FE model, a natural frequency of 1.2 Hz was obtained for the first mode shape of the tower. In addition, the FE model showed that consideration of the first three mode shapes of the tower resulted in the contribution of 96% of tower's seismic mass. Pushover analysis was employed to investigate the seismic performance of the tower. Results indicated that slabs were the most vulnerable structural components in the tower. They found that high stresses mostly concentrated at the corner of slabs where they were connected to the wings. At these locations, large deformations were observed in slabs. It was also reported that wings responded to the lateral loads independently and the slabs were incapable of providing a rigid diaphragm in order to make them work together. Results also showed that, since the majority of seismic mass concentrated at wings, the lumped mass approximation method employed by design engineers was not suitable for modeling the dynamic behavior of the tower.

It is worth mentioning that, in this study, the control cab was not simulated explicitly in the FE model, therefore, no result was provided for its seismic behavior. Moreover, usage of a fixed-base FE model, as shown by Vafaei et al. [8], may underestimate seismic induced damages to the mid-height of the tower. In addition, pushover analysis employed in this study may not provide reliable results for ATC towers [8].

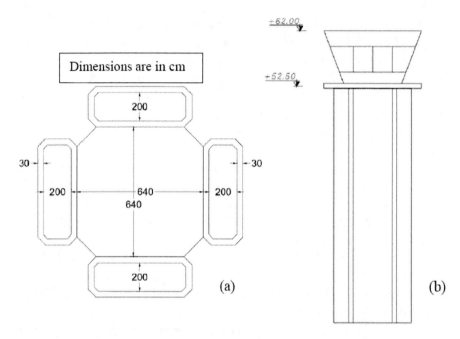

Figure 6. (a) Plan of the ATC tower. (b) Elevation view of the ATC tower.

In another study, Vafaei et al. [8] employed linear and nonlinear analysis in order to investigate seismic vulnerability of a tall air traffic control tower through numerical simulations. The studied ATC tower had 120 m height and took advantage of a concrete core to resist lateral loads. The thickness of the concrete core varied from 1.00 m at the foundation level to 0.61 m at the top level. The tower rested on a 3 m thick mat foundation which was supported by 57 concrete piles with the length of 30 m. The established FE model considered two different simulation scenarios. At first, supports at the base of the tower were assumed to be fixed. In the second model, the foundation and piles were included in the FE model in order to investigate the effect of soil-pile-foundation interaction on the seismic behavior of the tower. Figure 7 displays the established FE models in PERFORM-3D [9] software. A natural frequency of 0.35 Hz was obtained for the first mode shape of the tower. This value was validated experimentally through measuring the response of the tower under wind excitation. Nonlinear behavior of concrete walls was simulated using fiber method. Lumped plastic hinge method was used to account for the inelastic behavior of beams and columns. The employed linear analysis included equivalent static method together with response spectrum approach. For studying nonlinear behavior of the tower, pushover and nonlinear time history analysis were used. Results indicated that linear and pushover analysis underestimated the base shear of the tower when compared with the results of nonlinear time history analysis. In addition, shear force distribution along the height of the tower was dissimilar between linear and nonlinear methods. Comparison between fixed-base model and the model inclusive of soil-pile-foundation interaction revealed that damage to the mid-height of the tower was underestimated by the fixed-base model. This signified the inclusion of soil-pile-foundation interaction in the FE model. They also reported that response spectrum analysis was able to estimate the maximum displacement of the tower with a good precision when compared with the results of nonlinear time history analysis. On the other hand, pushover analysis and equivalent linear method, respectively, slightly underestimated and significantly overestimated it.

Although results of this study showed the importance of inclusion of the effect of soil-pile-foundation interaction in the FE model of ATC tower, its importance for midrise and short towers need to be investigated by other case studies. Similarly, the accuracy of pushover analysis results, which through this study was demonstrated to be not sufficient for the ATC towers, need to be investigated for shorter towers.

A wall-frame ATC tower with the total height of 30m was studied by Moravej et al. [10]. As shown in Figure 8, the lateral load resisting system of the tower consisted of an inner concrete core with the total height of 22.2 m, an outer concrete core with the total height of 11.6 m and a moment resisting frame throughout the height of the tower. From the finite element model, the natural period of the first mode shape was estimated 0.69 sec. As shown in Figure 8(b), the fifth mode shape of the tower imposed significant bending to the columns of equipment rooms. It is evident that the inner core is finished below this level. Therefore, the lateral stiffness of this level suddenly faces a great reduction compared to the level below. This in return imposes its effect to the fifth mode shape of the tower. It is noteworthy that, this observation is similar to the failure mechanism of the ATC tower of Qeshm International Airport, Iran, as it was discussed in the previous section. Consideration of the first 35 mode shapes assured attaining to 90% mass participation ratio for both principal directions. Moravej et al. [10] employed 14 natural earthquake records in order to run a series of nonlinear time history analysis. A comparison was made between results of linear (i.e., equivalent static and response spectrum analysis) and nonlinear analysis. It was found that the mean inelastic drift ratios obtained from nonlinear time history analysis followed a similar pattern to that of linear analyses. Results of linear and nonlinear analysis also displayed a similar pattern for shear force distribution in the outer core, however, for inner core linear analysis failed to predict a correct pattern for shear force distribution along the height of the tower. A displacement amplification factor of 2.6 was suggested for the estimation of inelastic displacement of the tower when using linear analysis. Results also showed that the overturning moment at the base of the tower was significantly underestimated by the linear analysis, therefore, a larger safety factor against overturning was required.

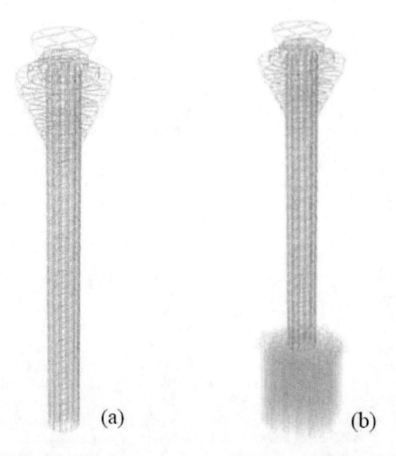

Figure 7. FE models of 120 m tall ATC tower. (a) Fixed-base model. (b) Soil-piles-foundation model.

Similar to the first case study (i.e., Eshghi and Farrokhi [6]), herein, the FE model did not account for the effect of soil-foundation interaction. However, unlike the first case study that required only the first three mode shapes, herein, the first 35 mode shapes required led to the 90% participation of seismic mass. This clearly indicates the significant difference in the dynamic behavior of ATC towers.

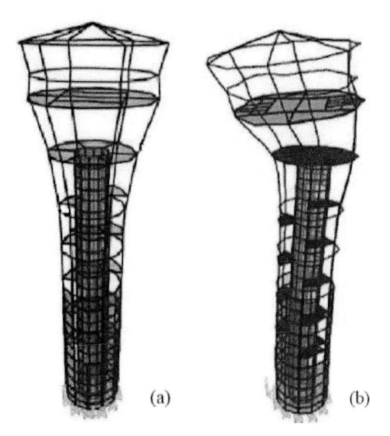

Figure 8. (a) Finite element model of a wall-frame ATC tower. (b) The fifth mode shape of the tower.

Muthukumar and Sabelli [11] studied seismic behavior of a 60 m tall ATC tower at San Francisco Airport, USA. The tower relied on a concrete core against lateral loads. The thickness of the concrete core for the first 15.6 m height of the tower was 0.76 m and for the rest was 0.45m. The tower also made use of a vertical post-tensioning system to provide self-centering during major earthquakes. A performance-based design approach was employed to investigate seismic behavior of the tower under suites of ground motion records scaled to the Maximum Considered Earthquake (MCE) and Design Basis Earthquake (DBE) levels. Two target performance objectives were selected for the tower. These two objectives included Immediate Occupancy (IO) at the DBE level and Collapse Prevention (CP) at the MCE level. In addition, the maximum drift of the tower at DBE and MCE levels were limited to 0.02 and 0.03 story height, respectively. The finite element model of the tower was established in PERFORM-3D software [12] considering the mat foundation of the tower and piles beneath it. The concrete core was designed such that the main source of the inelastic drift of the tower to be the formation of plastic hinge slightly above the level where the change in the thickness of the wall occurred. Results of nonlinear time history analysis indicated that a controlled seismic performance was achieved through this specific design. The tower showed the maximum seismic demand at the designated plastic hinge region. In addition, drifts along the height of the tower were all below the considered thresholds. It was also observed that the force-controlled actions in the structural components exhibited acceptable performance.

Currently, the performance-based design approach is the most reliable method for the seismic design of complex structures like ATC towers. Through this approach, design engineers can make sure that the structural system reaches to design targets and performance objectives that have been defined for them. However, besides many advantages that this sophisticated design approach has, it comes with some drawbacks. The main issue with performance-based design approach is that this method is inherently a controlling approach rather than being a design method. In other words, before this method can be applied to a structure all structural elements should be designed and their size and other specifications should be determined. Moreover, this method is time-consuming and costly.

Wilcoski and Heymsfield [13] worked on the rehabilitation of type L FAA airport traffic control tower at San Carlos, California, USA. The structural system of the type L ATC tower consisted of four inverted L-shaped reinforced concrete columns connected to each other below the control cab together with a steel moment resisting frame for forming its control cab. The height of the tower at the base of control cab was 9 m. The finite element model of the tower was established in SAP2000 software. For seismic evaluation of the tower, a similar procedure to that of FEMA 273 [14] was adopted. In order to analyze the tower, response spectrum analysis was employed. In addition, seismic hazard was set to the maximum considered earthquake (MCE) level. The performance objective of structural elements at

MCE level was considered to be life safety level. Results indicated a high demand to capacity ratio for the base plates of control cab columns leading to their failure during ground motions. Therefore, a retrofitting plan comprising of welding tube members to the base of each column in a pentagon configuration was suggested. Further investigation showed that the proposed retrofit plan reduced the drift within the control cab and decreased the demand to capacity ratio of base plates to an acceptable range.

Findings of this research clearly indicate that even short ATC towers can be vulnerable against seismic actions. Moreover, this study also emphasizes on the seismic vulnerability of control cabs which is similar to findings of other researchers. It is noteworthy that, the linear approach (i.e., response spectrum analysis) used for the analysis of this short ATC tower has been capable of displaying the weakness of structural system at the control cab level. However, other researchers have shown that linear approaches may not estimate the seismic response of tall ATC towers accurately.

Vafaei et al. [15] worked on the seismic design response factors of three force-based designed ATC towers. All of the studied towers had an inner and an outer concrete core to resist lateral loads. In addition, all towers took advantage of a steel moment resisting frame for construction of their control cab and junction levels. The height of towers varied from 23.7 m to 51.7 m. All towers rested on a mat foundation with a thickness ranging from 1.2 m for the shortest tower to 1.5 m for the tallest tower. The thickness of inner core of all towers was 0.25 m with a reinforcement ratio of 0.25%. The outer core of towers had a thickness of 0.4 m except for the tallest tower that was 0.45m. The reinforcement ratio of the outer concrete cores varied from 0.42% to 1.7%. The finite element models of ATC towers were established in PERFORM 3D software [12] including the effect of soil-foundation interaction. Results of modal analysis displayed a natural period of 0.44 sec for the shortest, 1.81 sec for the tallest and 1.05 sec. for the midrise tower. In addition to pushover analysis, towers were subjected to a series of nonlinear time history analysis using 14 natural earthquake records. Results indicated that the employed response modification factor (R-factor) for the design of the shortest tower was very conservative. However, for the tallest tower, the calculated R-factor was significantly smaller than the employed design R-factor. This indicated that the height of ATC towers has a great impact on their seismic vulnerability. As the height increased, the seismic vulnerability of ATC towers was also increased. In addition, results indicated that considering a displacement amplification of 4 was appropriate for all studied towers.

The importance of this study is because of providing an estimation of the response modification factor of ATC towers. As mentioned earlier, in order to employ advanced seismic design methods (i.e., performance-based design), often an initial design of structural elements should be carried out in advance. This initial design often follows a force-based design method that requires a conservative estimation of response modification factors. Current seismic design codes do not provide any guidance about R-factor of ATC towers. Therefore, this study can help design engineers to have an estimation on this factor for their design. It should be mentioned that, although this study has focused on the R-factor of ATC towers, since it includes only concrete wall lateral load resisting system, more research on the R-factor of other structural system are required.

RECOMMENDATION FOR FUTURE STUDIES

It is evident from the existing literature that, the published materials on the seismic design and vulnerability of ATC towers have been limited. This signifies an urgent need for more research in this field. One main reason for such urgent studies is the important role that ATC towers and airports play in disaster mitigation. In addition to this, the diversity of structural systems that have been employed for ATC towers in order to suit their architectural design has made the dynamic behavior of each tower unique. The differences in the mass and stiffness distribution of the structural systems of ATC towers are the main reason for such unique dynamic response. Besides, many of old ATC towers have not been designed for seismic actions or their seismic design has been based on a force-based concept which is obviously not appropriate for important structures like ATC towers. Therefore, authors believed that at the first place a seismic design guideline that specifically has been tailored to deal with the unique dynamic characteristics of ATC towers should be developed. The guideline should be able to address the following matters:

1) What is the appropriate drift limit for ATC towers?

Unlike common buildings where an identical drift limit is selected for all stories, upper levels of ATC tower specially the control cab should have a smaller allowable drift in order to minimize damage to non-structural components like glasses that cover their perimeter.

2) What is the appropriate empirical equation to estimate the natural period of ATC towers?

Current seismic design codes suggest empirical equations for design engineers to estimate with a good precision the natural period of buildings and some non-building structures. However, so far, such empirical equations have not been developed for ATC towers. Therefore, in the current practice, estimation of natural period of ATC towers relies only on the FE models. As it was shown by researchers [8] if FE models do not include the effect of soil-foundation-structure interaction into account, the calculated natural period may not be accurate enough. On the other hand, the inclusion of the effect of soil-foundation-structure interaction makes the analysis more complicated and sensitive to the variables used in the model. Therefore, the presence of empirical equations can enhance the reliability of calculated natural frequencies through FE models.

3) What are the appropriate coefficients for estimating effective shear and flexural stiffness of ATC towers?

As mentioned earlier, many of ATC towers employ concrete walls as their main lateral load resisting system because of their higher stiffness. For a linear analysis, design engineers should have a good estimation on the effective shear and flexural stiffness of concrete walls and other reinforced concrete elements when they establish the FE model of ATC towers. Design codes like ACI 318-14 [16] have recommended some coefficients to reduce the shear and flexural stiffness of structural elements calculated based on their gross sections in order to account for parameters that reduce their stiffness before and during earthquakes. It is important to have recommendations for calculation of effective stiffness of structural elements in ATC towers.

4) When the effect of soil-pile-foundation interaction should be included in the FE models?

It was seen that the effect of soil-pile-foundation interaction was significant in the tall ATC tower as it had influences on the damage intensity at the mid-height of the tower. Therefore, it should be determined when it is necessary to include the effect of such interaction into the FE models.

5) What is the appropriate equation for estimating shear force distribution along the height of ATC towers?

The initial seismic design of buildings is often based on a simple equation that provides an estimation on how seismic forces are distributed along the height of structures. Such equations that can determine with a good precision the shear force distribution along the height of buildings have been presented in many seismic codes for buildings [17]. However, the accuracy of these equations for estimation of shear force distribution in ATC towers need to be investigated.

6) What are the appropriate performance objectives and acceptance criteria for the seismic design of ATC towers?

It was mentioned that the performance-based design approach is a suitable method for seismic design of ATC towers. However, appropriate selection of performance objectives and defining their acceptance criteria need a comprehensive guideline. It is also important to investigate how much devices used inside ATC towers are sensitive to acceleration, velocity and displacement before defining their acceptance criteria against seismic actions.

Although many more matters may be needed to be addressed in addition to what have been mentioned above, authors believe that the above-mentioned issues are the most critical matters for the seismic design and evaluation of ATC towers. It is noteworthy that, addressing the above-mentioned matters needs much more research to be conducted and obviously it will take a lot of efforts and time.

REFERENCES

[1] https://www.usca.es/en/profession/history-of-air-traffic-control/.
[2] FAA, Federal Aviation Administration (2004); Airport traffic control tower and terminal radar approach control – facility design guidelines.
[3] ICAO, International Civil Aviation Organization (1984); Air traffic services planning manual – Doc 9426-AN/924. https://panethos.word press.com/2014/02/22/worlds-sky-high-civilian-air-traffic-control-towers/.

[4]   Hartmann, J. H. (2014). Feasibility study of Air Traffic Control Towers around the globe: International research regarding the local influences providing an optimal structural design for air traffic control towers around the globe in an economical perspective, Master thesis, TU Delft, Delft University of Technology. http://resolver.tudelft.nl/uuid:d967d34 b-09ad-490e-94d6-66bc3a30d9c9.

[5]   http://www.seattlepi.com/local/komo/article/Glass-from-Sea-Tac-tower-breaks-in-D-C-quake-2138101.php.

[6]   Eshghi, S., & Farrokhi, H. (2003). Seismic Vulnerability Analysis of Airport Traffic Control Towers. *Journal of Seismology and Earthquake Engineering,* 5(1), 31.

[7]   ANSYS. References and Manuals: Basic Analysis Procedures Guide "ANSYS Advanced Analysis Techniques Guide-ANSYS Operation GuideANSYS Modeling & Meshing Guide-ANSYS Structural Analysis Guide- ANSYS Commands Reference-ANSYS Elements Reference-ANSYS Theory Reference ANSYS V.5.40, ANSYS Co. (1997), 9th Edition SAS IP Inc.

[8]   Vafaei, M., Adnan, A. B., & Rahman, A. B. A. (2014). Seismic performance evaluation of an airport traffic control tower through linear and nonlinear analysis. *Structure and Infrastructure Engineering,* 10(8), 963-975.

[9]   Computers and Structures, Inc. (2006). Perform 3D-Version 4: Nonlinear analysis and performance assessment for 3d structures, User Guide. Berkeley, CA: Computer and Structures, Inc.

[10]   Moravej, H., Vafaei, M., & Abu, B. (2016). Seismic performance of a wall-frame air traffic control tower. *Earthquakes and Structures*, 10(2), 463-482.

[11]   Muthukumar, S., & Sabelli, R. (2013). Nonlinear Seismic Analysis of a Round Concrete Tower with a Post-Tensioned Self-Centering System. In *Structures Congress 2013: Bridging Your Passion with Your Profession* (pp. 2128-2139). ASCE.

[12]   Computers and Structures, Inc. (CSI) (2010). Perform-3D – Nonlinear Analysis and Performance Assessment for 3D Structures, v5.0.0, Berkeley, CA.

[13]   Wilcoski, J., & Heymsfield, E. (2002). Performance and rehabilitation of type L FAA airport traffic control tower at San Carlos, California, for seismic loading. *Journal of performance of constructed facilities*, 16(2), 85-93.

[14] Federal Emergency Management Agency (FEMA) (1997). "NEHRP guidelines (FEMA 273) and commentary (FEMA 274) for the seismic rehabilitation of buildings." Federal Emergency Management Agency, Washington, D.C.

[15] Vafaei, M., & Alih, S. C. (2016). Assessment of seismic design response factors of air traffic control towers. *Bulletin of Earthquake Engineering,* 14(12), 3441-3461.

[16] ACI 318-14 & PCA (2014) Notes on 318-14: Building code requirements for structural concrete and commentary. American Concrete Institute.

[17] ASCE, SEI 7–10 (2010) Minimum design loads for buildings and other structures. *American Society of Civil Engineers* (ASCE), Reston.

BIOGRAPHICAL SKETCHES

Mohammadreza Vafaei

Mohammadreza Vafaei (Ph.D., P.Eng., M.ASCE, M.EERI, M.SSA) is currently a Senior Lecturer in the Faculty of Civil Engineering, Universiti Teknologi Malaysia (UTM), and a research fellow of Forensic Engineering Center,UTM. As a professional engineer, he has served many consultant companies and he has led seismic design of many mega structures including tall residential and office buildings, airport terminals, air traffic control towers, lattice telecommunication towers, bridges, water reservoirs and monumental structures. His expertise includes seismic design of special structures, seismic retrofit, damage identification and structural health monitoring systems. Dr. Vafaei has published many reseach articles in the field of seisicm vulnerability of ATC towers and damage identifcation in refered journals and conferences. He has also invented new devices for mitigtion of seismic-induced damages to structures.

Affiliation: *Faculty of Civil Engineering, Universiti Teknologi Malaysia (UTM)*

Education: *Ph.D. in earthquake engineering from UTM*

Business Address: *Faculty of Civil Engineering, Universiti Teknologi Malaysia (UTM), 81310, Johor, Malaysia*

Research and Professional Experience:

1. Seismic Vulnerability Study of Special Structures
2. Performance-based Seismic Design
3. Structural Health Monitoring Systems
4. Neural networks and Wavelet Transforms for Damage Identification of Structures

Professional Appointments: *Senior Lecturer*

Honors:

Editor for Journals

1. Editorial board for the International Journal of Civil Engineering and Building Materials.
2. Editorial board for Journal of Structural Engineering and Management.
3. Editorial board for Recent Trends in Civil Engineering and Technology.

Reviewer for Journals and Conferences

1. Reviewer for the Journal of Structure and Infrastructure Engineering.
2. Reviewer for Bulletin of Earthquake Engineering Journal.
3. Reviewer for Construction and Building Materials Journal.
4. Reviewer for Journal Teknologi.
5. Reviewer for Malaysian Journal of Civil Engineering.
6. Reviewer for the International Journal of Electrical Power and Energy Systems.
7. Reviewer for 2011 International Conference on Civil Engineering and Building Materials (2011 CEBM) Kunming, China, July 29-31, 2011.
8. Reviewer for International Conference on Advanced Science, Engineering and Technology (ICASET) 2015, Pulau Pinang, Malaysia.

Scientific Committee and Editorial Board of International Conferences

1. Editorial Board for the "The Fourth International Conference on Soft Computing Technology in Civil, Structural and Environmental Engineering." Prague, Czech Republic, 1-4 September 2015.
2. Technical Committee of International Conference on Design and Manufacturing Engineering (ICDME2016), Auckland, New Zealand during July 4-6, 2016.
3. International Scientific Committee of Advances in Civil Engineering and Building Materials, Peer Reviewed papers from 2th International Conference on Civil Engineering and Building Materials (CEBM 2012), 17-18 November, Hong Kong.
4. International Scientific Committee of Advances in Civil Engineering and Building Materials, Peer Reviewed papers from 3rd International Conference on Civil Engineering and Building Materials (CEBM 2013), 7-8 December, Hong Kong.
5. International Scientific Committee of Advances in Civil Engineering and Building Materials IV, Peer Reviewed papers from 4th International Conference on Civil Engineering and Building Materials (CEBM 2014), 15-17 November, Hong Kong.
6. Technical Committee of 2016 International Conference on Frontiers of Composite Materials (ICFCM2016), 19-21 November, Auckland, New Zealand.
7. Technical Committee of International Conference on Mechanics, Civil Engineering and Building Material [MCEBM2017], 21-23 April 2017, Nanjing, China.

Invited Speaker (International)

1. Invited Speaker for Collaborative Conference on Earthquake Science and Engineering (CCESE 2015), 15-18 September, Chengdu, China.
2. Invited Speaker for International Conference on Design and Manufacturing Engineering (ICDME2016), 4-6 July, Auckland, New Zealand.
3. Invited Speaker for Collaborative Conference on Earthquake Science and Engineering (CCESE 2016), 4-8 September, Budapest, Hungary.

Invited Speaker (National)

1) Geotechnical Earthquake Engineering in Malaysia, 1-2 March 2016, Kuala Lumpur. –Organized by Ministry of Works Malaysia.
2) Tall Buildings and Their Design Challenges, 23rd February 2016. Johor Bahru. -Organized by Center for Forensic Engineering.
3) Seismic Design of Structures in Accordance with Eurocode 8, 6-7 November, 2015, Johor Bahru. –Organized by The Institution of Engineers Malaysia, IEM, Southern Branch.
4) Structural Investigations on Damaged Buildings due to Sabah Earthquake and Available Retrofit Strategies, 1st August, 2015, Johor Bahru. –Organized by The Institution of Engineers Malaysia (IEM) Southern Branch.
5) 2015 Sabah Earthquake; Structural Forensic Investigations and Retrofit Strategies, 9th July 2015, Kuala Lumpur. –Organized by Public Works Department, PWD.
6) Health Monitoring of Civil Structures. 3rd October 2015. Johor Bahru, Universiti Teknologi Malaysia. –Organized by Center for Forensic Engineering.
7) Seismic Design of Structures, Eurocode, Performance Based Design and Fragility Curves. 5-6 March 2014, Kuala Lumpur. –Organized by Malaysian Structural Steel Association.
8) Performance Based Seismic Design. 21-22 January 2014, Johor Bahru. –Organized by UTM Engineering Seismology and Earthquake Engineering Research Group.
9) ANSYS Training Workshop & IT Application in Civil Engineering. 7-8 March 2014, Johor Bahru. –Organized by Universiti Teknologi Malaysia.

Publications from the Last 3 Years:

Vafaei, M., C. Alih, Sophia (2017). Adequacy of First Mode Shape Differences for Damage Identification Using Neural Networks. *Neural Computing and Application.* DOI: 10.1007/s00521-017-2846-6.

Vafaei, M., & Alih, S. C. (2016). Assessment of seismic design response factors of air traffic control towers. *Bulletin of Earthquake Engineering,* *14*(12), 3441-3461.

Shad, H., Adnan, A., Behbahani, H., **Vafaei, M.**, (2016) Efficiency of TLDs with Bottom-Mounted Baffles in Suppression of Structural Responses.

Structural Engineering and Mechanics, an International Journal. 60 (1), 131-148. DOI: 10.12989/sem.2016.60.1.131

Behbahani, H., Adnan, A., **Vafaei, M,** Ong Peng P., Shad, H. (2016). Effects of TLCD with maneuverable flaps on vibration control of a SDOF structure. *Meccanica.* DOI 10.1007/s11012-016-0473-4.

Behbahani, H., Adnan, A., **Vafaei, M,** Ong Peng P., Shad, H. (2016).Vibration Mitigation of Structures through TLCD with Embedded Baffles. Experimental Mechanics. DOI: 10.1007/s40799-016-0163-0.

Vafaei, M., C. Alih, Sophia. (2015) Influence of Higher Order Modes and Mass Configuration on the Damage Detection via Wavelet Analysis. *Earthquake and Structures.* 9(6) 1221-1232.

Vafaei, M., C. Alih, Sophia (2015) Ideal Strain Gage Placement for Seismic Health Monitoring of Structures. *Earthquake and Structures.* 8(3), 541-553.

Vafaei, M., Azlan, A., Alih S., Ahamd Baharuddin, A.R. (2015) A Wavelet-based Technique for Damage Quantification via Mode Shape Decomposition. *Journal of structure and infrastructure engineering.* *11*(7), 869-883. DOI:10.1080/15732479.2014.917114.

Vafaei, M., Azlan, A., Ahamd Baharuddin, A.R.(2014). A Neuro-Wavelet Technique for Seismic Damage Identification of Cantilever Structures. *Journal of structure and infrastructure engineering.* *10*(12), 1666-1684. DOI:10.1080/15732479.2013.849746.

Vafaei, M., Azlan, A., (2014). Seismic Damage Detection of Tall Airport Traffic Control Towers Using Wavelet Analysis. *Journal of structure and infrastructure engineering.* *10*(1), 106-127 DOI:10.1080/ 15732479.2012.704051.

Vafaei, M., Azlan, A., Ahamd Baharuddin, A.R., (2014). Seismic Performance Evaluation of an Airport Traffic Control Tower through Linear and Nonlinear Analysis. *Journal of Structure and Infrastructure Engineering.* *10*(8), 963-975. **DOI:**10.1080/15732479.2013.774030.

Vafaei, M., C. Alih, Sophia, (2015), Seismic Vulnerability of Air Traffic Control Towers, *Collaborative Conference on Earthquake Science and Engineering, CCESE,* Chengdu, China.

Vafaei, M., C. Alih, Sophia, (2015), Seismic Detailing; A Compromised Principal for Seismic Design in Malaysia, *9th Asia Pacific Structural Engineering and Construction Conference (APSEC),* Kuala Lumpur, Malaysia.

Vafaei, M., Sophia C Alih, Ali Fallah, (2016) Seismic Performance of an Innovative Beam-To-Column Connection for Precast Structures,

Collaborative Conference on Earthquake Science and Engineering (CCESE 2016), 4-8 September 2016, Budapest Hungary.

Sophia C. Alih, **Vafaei, M.**, Nufail Bin Ismail, (2016) *Collaborative Conference on Earthquake Science and Engineering* (CCESE 2016), 4-8 September 2016, Budapest Hungary.

Sophia C. Alih

Affiliation:

Faculty of Civil Engineering, Institute of Noise and Vibration, Universiti Teknologi Malaysia, Johor Bahru, Johor Malaysia.

Education:

Doctor of Philosophy (Civil Engineering)

Business Address:

Department of Structure and Materials, Faculty of Civil Engineering, Universiti Teknologi Malaysia, 81310 Johor Bahru, Johor Malaysia.

Research and Professional Experience:

Sophia C. Alih (PhD) is currently a Senior Lecturer in the Department of Structure and Materials, Faculty of Civil Engineering, UTM JB and a research associate of Institute of Noise and Vibration, UTM. Apart from her academic profession, she has been involved in several consultancy projects for bridge and building inspection in East and West Malaysia since 2004. Her expertise include structural dynamic analysis and design, structural inspection for seismic induced damages, structural retrofit, steel structures, and material sciences. She has been also supervising research works of five PhD and four Master candidates.

Professional Appointments:

Senior Lecturer

Honors:

Educational Committee Member of Malaysian Structural Steel Association

Invited Speaker for the *Collaborative Conference on Earthquake Science and Engineering* 2016 Invited Speaker for the Seminar on the Geotechnical Earthquake Engineering in Malaysia, 2016

Editorial Board Member for Canadian Arena of Applied Scientific Research

Editorial Board Member for STM Journal

Reviewer for International Journal of Technology

Publications from the Last 3 Years:

1. Vafaei, M., **C. Alih, Sophia.** (2016). Assessment of Seismic Design Response Factors of Air Traffic Control Towers. Bulletin of Earthquake Engineering. **14** (12) 3441–3461.
2. Vafaei, M., **Alih, C. S.,** Abdul Rahman, Q. (2016). Drift Demands of Low-Ductile Moment Resistance Frames (Mrf) Under Far Field Earthquake Excitations Considering Soft-Storey Phenomenon. *Journal Teknologi*. **78** (6), 82–92.
3. Vafaei, M., **C. Alih, Sophia** (2017). Adequacy of First Mode Shape Differences for Damage Identification Using Neural Networks. *Neural Computing and Application.* (In-press).
4. Vafaei, M., **C. Alih, Sophia** (2015). Influence of Higher Order Modes and Mass Configuration on the Damage Detection via Wavelet Analysis. Earthquake and Structures. **9** (6) 1221-1232.
5. Vafaei, M., Azlan, A., **Alih S.,** Ahamd Baharuddin, A.R. (2014) A Wavelet-based Technique for Damage Quantification via Mode Shape Decomposition. *Journal of Structure and Infrastructure Engineering.* **11**, 869-883.
6. Vafaei, M., **C. Alih, Sophia** (2014). Ideal Strain Gage Placement for Seismic Health Monitoring of Structures. *Earthquake and Structures.* **8**, 541-553.
7. Nufail Bin Ismail, **Sophia C. Alih***, Mohammadreza Vafaei, (2016). Performance of Novel Hybrid Damper for Structural Dynamic Response Reduction, 1st Proceeding of Civil Engineering Structure & Materials. **1**(1), 41-54.
8. Vafaei, M., **C. Alih, Sophia,** (2015), Seismic Vulnerability of Air Traffic Control Towers, *Collaborative Conference on Earthquake Science and Engineering, CCESE,* Chengdu, China.
9. Vafaei, M., **C. Alih, Sophia,** (2015), Seismic Detailing; A Compromised Principal for Seismic Design in Malaysia, *9th Asia Pacific Structural Engineering and Construction Conference (APSEC),* Kuala Lumpur, Malaysia.

10. Mohammadreza Vafaei*, **Sophia C Alih**, Ali Fallah, Seismic Performance of an Innovative Beam-To-Column Connection for Precast Structures, *Collaborative Conference on Earthquake Science and Engineering* (CCESE 2016), 4-8 September 2016, Budapest Hungary.

11. **Sophia C. Alih***, Mohammadreza Vafaei, Nufail Bin Ismail, *Collaborative Conference on Earthquake Science and Engineering* (CCESE 2016), 4-8 September 2016, Budapest Hungary.

12. **Sophia C Alih***, Mohammadreza Vafaei, Or Tan Teng and Farnoud Rahimi Mansour, Production of Rubber-based Damper for Construction Industry in Malaysia, *3rd National Conference on Knowledge Transfer* (NCKT'16), 30 Nov-1 Dec 2016, Penang.

13. **Sophia C. Alih** (2016), Intelligent Bridge Inspection Rating, LAP Lambert Academic Publishing.

In: Aviation and Airport Security
Editor: Don Lawrence

ISBN: 978-1-53611-909-1
© 2017 Nova Science Publishers, Inc.

Chapter 2

EMPLOYMENT IMPACTS OF THE BERLIN BRANDENBURG AIRPORT "WILLY BRANDT": THE APPLICATION OF SCENARIO TECHNIQUES DURING THE PLANNING PROCESS

Dieter Bogai[1], and Franziska Hirschenauer[2]*

[1]Institute for Employment Research —
Regional Research Network Berlin-Brandenburg, Berlin, Germany
[2]Institute for Employment Research —
Research Institute of the German Federal Employment Agency,
Nuremberg, Germany

ABSTRACT

The construction of a new single airport for the capital of Germany has an erratic history that dates back to the early nineties. After several postponements in putting the airport into operation, its opening is now projected for the course of the year 2018. During the long planning period the employment impacts of a major airport played an important role in the public dialogue. This paper sets out how a scenario technique was used to calculate employment effects related to this major airport project.

* Institute for Employment Research, Friedrichstr. 34, D-10969 Berlin, Germany. Email: dieter.bogai@iab.de.

The first assessment approach was utilized to examine alternative sites for the new single airport in the early planning stage. It found that the location of Schönefeld, the site which was finally chosen, would generate the highest effects on employment among the three alternative proposals of suitable sites. The reasons were its short distance to the metropolis of Berlin and its greatest stimulating effects on economic growth in the surrounding area.

The second assessment approach was performed three years before in 2008, prior to the expected opening date of the airport. The mission was to identify industries, occupations and regions in Berlin and Brandenburg that would benefit from air transport services. Based on this information, qualification measures should be developed. In contrast to the usual quantification framework of magnitudes the assessment concentrated on structural changes in employment. The procedure is based on the employment statistics that contains 336 occupations and which is able to map the regional development of air transport related employment in 402 German districts. The employment figures are differentiated according to jobs that are directly located at the airport site, indirect employment effects in the aerospace industry and in related sectors and catalytic effects on the economy as a whole.

The results give evidence for direct and indirect employment effects outside the airport site in Berlin, and for regional effects in the southern districts of Berlin, notably in the counties of Dahme-Spreewald, Teltow-Fläming and Potsdam. It was predicted that aircraft-related industries located in the administrative district of Dahme-Spreewald stimulate the job creation in technical occupations in Brandenburg. The most tentative forecast is related to occupations that benefit from better airport infrastructure via catalytic effects. Those impacts especially were found for service occupations with university degrees such as consultants and managers which are located in Berlin and in the metropolitan areas in Brandenburg.

Keywords: airport, employment, scenario technique

INTRODUCTION

The construction of a new single airport for the capital of Germany has an eventful history which was controversial with regard to the geographic site, the environmental impacts and the organization of construction. After the opening date has been postponed several times, the opening is expected to be in 2018.

First planning of a single airport for the capital region Berlin Brandenburg dates back to the early nineties. During the long planning period the employment impacts of a major airport played an important role in the public dialogue because of adverse economic conditions in the post transformation period accompanied by a substantial destruction of jobs in Berlin and Brandenburg. Moreover new jobs were a compensating argument for the annoyances of operation. The Institute for Employment Research (IAB), the research institute of the federal employment agency, was firstly involved in an early stage of planning when three alternative sites at which the airport could have been located were discussed. Fifteen years later, prior to the first announced opening date, the government of Brandenburg assigned the IAB to evaluate conceivable employment effects of the airport project. This topic was important for local politicians because the unemployment rates in Berlin and Brandenburg were persistently higher than the German average (Blien/Hirschenauer 1994). Additionally, productivity figures like gross domestic product per capita were lower in Berlin compared to the national average - a fact not realized in any other European capital (GLE 2003). In order to identify concrete points of intervention for the labor market strategy we developed a procedure that focuses on occupational and regional effects regarding the major job impacts induced by the operation of the airport.

This paper is organized as follows. First, those milestones in the history of the airport are introduced that play a major role in understanding the never ending problems of finishing the construction process and the unlimited growth of costs. Then, a first rough calculation for the airport´s employment effects for the three alternative building sites considered in 1994 is presented that could have played a role in the early decision-making process as the current report of the House of Representatives (2016: 79) stated. Within the mandate from the government of Brandenburg in 2008 the impact channels of the airport infrastructure on regional and national employment were evaluated. Irrespective of the quantitative accuracy of the calculated employment effects it could be expected that there are branches and occupations that benefit from a single airport in the Berlin Brandenburg area. Therefore, we developed a pragmatic approach in order to give politicians an advice for qualification measures for the workforce. This task was of significance also for the employment office because of the high unemployment rate in the Berlin Brandenburg region. Methodologically, the framework is based on a comparative analysis considering the most important German agglomerations with international airports. They provide a basis for developing scenarios about the occupation-specific employment effects for the Berlin Brandenburg airport. We conclude this article emphasizing the importance of an appropriate airport infrastructure in the greater region of the German capital which achieved an economic turnaround about ten years ago after a long period of radical structural change and stagnation in Gross Domestic Product.

1. HISTORICAL BACKGROUND OF PLANNING A SINGLE AIRPORT BERLIN BRANDENBURG

At the end of the division of Europe in 1989 the Berlin airport system reflected the unique historical circumstances originated from the bipolar world. The former western part of Berlin exhibited two airports directly in the city: Tempelhof airport the leading airport in Europe in the 1930ies and Tegel airport constructed in the 1970ies to expand the capacity that Tempelhof airport was unable to supply because of its location very close to extremely dense populated areas. The former German Democratic Republic used the central airport near to the town of Schönefeld in the state of Brandenburg that borders Berlin's southern boundary.

After German unification in 1990 first considerations of building a new single airport were made. Subsequently a long standing and erratic history of planning procedure and political disputes emerged. It took five years to find a location and further ten years before construction started. However, the controversies about the airport´s operation and its environmental impacts are not eliminated until now. In the end the construction of the Berlin Brandenburg Airport has suffered from continued delays. Until now, four official opening dates have not been met. At the beginning of this year the Governing Mayor of Berlin Michael Müller announced that the opening will not take place in 2017 either.

The history of events related to the airport started in 1990 when the red green government of Berlin decided not to expand the Tegel airport. Although there could easily be built a second terminal building that was allowed for in construction it was ruled out for environmental reasons. In 1991 several, partly odd places in the periphery of Brandenburg or even in the more remote districts in Sachsen-Anhalt or Poland came into play as possible locations for a new capital airport. In 1993 when the regional planning procedure for a new single airport Berlin Brandenburg International (BBI) was announced, three possible building sites remained in the procedure. The alternatives belonged to Sperenberg with already existing airfields for military use (48 km distant from Berlin Mitte - the city center of Berlin), Jüterbog-East (64 km distant from Berlin Mitte), and finally Schönefeld-South near by the existing airport

Schönefeld SXF (22 km distant from Berlin Mitte) which could be extended to a major international airport.

In that early planning procedure Schönefeld was qualified as an inappropriate location for an international airport because a huge number of inhabitants would have been affected by aviation noise (Berlin Brandenburg Airport Holding 1993; Maier 2008). The alternative sites located in less densely populated areas had the major advantage of operating 24 hours a day like the Leipzig airport nowadays. Later, after fixing the airport location, the operating hours became a controversial issue in public discussion and they were strongly restricted. In 1996 the politicians from Berlin and Brandenburg and the German Federal Ministry of Transportation finally agreed on a 'consensus decision' to build the new international airport Berlin Brandenburg "Willy Brandt" in Schönefeld using private investments. A major factor that led to the Schönefeld decision were the costs of public transport connection which was emphasized by the federal representative in the supervisory council of the airport. The costs of the remote airport locations in Brandenburg were too high to cover by the German Federal Ministry of Finance. In order to address concerns about the noise level of the airport, stricter regulations on the operating hours and noise insulation were imposed. It was planned to close the Tempelhof airport as soon as possible (effectively done in October 2008) and to cease the Tegel airport as soon as the new single airport opens.

In the course of the next ten years privatization failed and continuous court disputes between environmental interest groups and the airport holding at administrative courts prevented the start of construction (see for a complete description of events House of Representatives Berlin 2016). After several potential investors dropped out early in the bidding process, two bidding consortia emerged as serious contenders. Several juridical acts associated with a fair bidding procedure, led to the exclusion and reappointment of a consortium. Finally, both consortia teamed up and brought forth a plan for a joint offer in the year 2000. At that time, there was hope that the planning approval could be granted in 2002 including the opening of the airport in 2007. However, in 2001, the consortium of the two companies made its offer, which was significantly lower than expected. The Federal Minister of Transportation who formerly was the prime minister of Brandenburg declared that the offer would not meet the requirements, and in 2003 privatization was stopped. Both companies received a compensation payment of about €50 million for their planning effort.

Assuming that the investors hesitated because of the large risks involved in building the airport – it was still possible that lawsuits would stop the entire project – the airport holding considered building the airport with government loans and to privatize operation afterwards. Until 2006 several court judgments stopped the start of construction. Initially 3.300 later 4.000 complaints were submitted to the courts. In 2005, the Federal Administrative Court stopped the construction until a final decision about the opponent's claims would be reached. Such decision has never before been taken in the planning period of a large infrastructure project in German history. In March 2006, the Federal Administrative Court announced its final decision. It implies that citizens exposed to an average daily noise level above 62 decibels are entitled to receive compensation payments. Additionally, the court extended the area in which people have to receive sound-proof windows.

Regarding the air transport routes planned for the new airport a substantial change occurred shortly before the planned opening date. In September 2010 the German air-traffic control published aircraft arrival and departure paths for the Berlin Brandenburg airport, which significantly differed from earlier schedules used in the court decision for the construction permit. The Federal Administrative Court of Germany rejected a lawsuit on 31th of July 2012.

The current reasons for delaying the opening of the airport belong to the fire protection and the alarm system in the terminal building, which failed the mandatory acceptance test. In order to meet the requirements for the construction permit large scale reconstruction work of the fire system was needed. Meanwhile additional technical difficulties with the electronical control of the doors prevent timely opening. The project seems to raise costs endlessly. Originally, in 2006 the costs were estimated to reach about €2 billion. According to the finance executive of the state owned Airport Company of Berlin, Brandenburg and the Federal Republic of Germany € 4.3 billion were already spent in May 2015. The extra costs of construction until 2017 amount to € 2.5 billion. At the end of 2015 the European Commission conditioned the additional public subsidies to 2.2 billion €, so the total costs amount to 6.5 billion € three times more than initially planned.[1]

---

[1] http://www.tagesspiegel.de/berlin/flughafen-in-berlin-eu-begrenzt-ber-kosten-auf-6-5-milliarde n-euro/12728266.html [Airport-in-berlin-eu-limited-over-cost-on-6-5-billion-euro].

2. EMPLOYMENT MULTIPLIERS OF ALTERNATIVE AIRPORT LOCATIONS

As described in the previous chapter, three alternative locations for the Berlin Brandenburg airport were discussed throughout the planning procedure starting in 1993. The Governing Mayor of Berlin and the former President of the land employment office Berlin Brandenburg instructed the IAB to estimate the different employment effects for Sperenberg, Jüterbog and Schönefeld, the airport´s three potential building sites (Bogai/Wiethölter 1994). The results were delivered to the Governing Mayor of Berlin Eberhard Diepgen at the end of 1994.

At that time regional planning in Brandenburg were guided by the policy of a "decentralized concentration." Brandenburg is a region which comprises large rural areas with low population density. The economy suffered from poor economic development resulting from a misguided specialization initiated by the former socialist planners. Its economic structure was dominated by the steel industry and coal mining. Additionally, Brandenburg' economy was threatened by potential backwash effects triggering the flow of economic resources from peripheral areas to the agglomeration of Berlin, the economic hub located in the center of Brandenburg. So called urban development centers – central communes and their surroundings – were planned to emerge as the backbone of a polycentric development for the whole region (Ministry of Agriculture Brandenburg, Ministry of City Development Berlin 1999). The potential airport site Jüterbog was located in the center of regional growth Jüterbog/Luckenwalde in the urban belt surrounding Berlin. The Sperenberg site also in the near of such peripheral cities was qualified as a suitable location. But the former military use of the Russian army led to severe soil contamination and additional costs. The Schönefeld site is located near the center of the capital region potentially benefiting most from economic recovery of Berlin.

The labor market situation varied strongly across the three sites: The unemployment rate in the district of Königs-Wusterhausen to which the Schönefeld site belongs was 9.8 per cent in 1994 compared to 13.8 per cent in the region of Jüterbog. In Zossen the district where Sperenberg is located it was 11.1 per cent at that time. Taking into account that a significant part of the labor force participated in labor market programs, the de facto job deficit was much higher than indicated in the figures (Blien/Hirschenauer 1994). In contrast to the labor markets in Schönefeld and Sperenberg the region of

Jüterbog did not benefit much from commuters to Berlin. Moreover, the economic structure in the remote areas was more depressed by job losses during the transformation from a socialist economy into a free market society, especially in the overstaffed industrial and agricultural sector.

In addition to combating unemployment, the government of Brandenburg tried to reconstruct and revitalize degraded areas that arose from former industrial and military use. Land allocation and conversion of these polluted areas were closely linked to the development of a new economic structure. High and persistent unemployment rates in these areas reinforced by a greater distance to Berlin were key issues from the perspective of the Brandenburg government. These special problems considering regional policy in the stage of restructuring the former GDR economy should be kept in mind when considering the employment effects of the alternative airport sites.

The IAB analysis is founded on two main sources: the passenger forecasts of the Berlin Brandenburg airport holding were used and the assessment technique of employment figures was based on the records used in the planning procedure for the Franz-Josef-Strauß airport in Munich. Particularly the expertise of the ifo institute measuring the economic effects for the Munich area was taken into account.

At that time – the first half of the 1990ies – the state of the art of calculating employment effects was rather simple. It begins with calculating the direct effects – i.e., the number of employees on the airport site – depending on the number of passengers and tons of cargo. Indirect effects were defined through the supply and demand relationship between the airport and the indirectly employed through airport related businesses. The expertise from the ifo institute included a survey of employment multipliers, i.e., the ratio of indirect to direct employees related to different international airports during the 1980ies (Table 1). Those figures vary to a great extent. The high values of Zürich-Kloten II and III (15 minutes accessibility) depend on the very close to the airport located towns of Zürich and Kloten.

The positive multipliers for all airports indicate that they stimulate the economic activities in their surroundings. The strength of the stimulus depends on the vitality i.e., the economic strength already existing in the region. For the case of Berlin Brandenburg this aspect was emphasized by a study published in that time. The business consultancy Arthur D. Little and the German Institute of Economic Research (1993) stressed that the new airport would only have a significant positive impact on the regional economy if it was located close to the city of Berlin.

Table 1. Employment multipliers of selected international airports

Airport	Multiplier
Zürich-Kloten I	2.6
Zürich-Kloten II	3.0
Zürich-Kloten III	4.0
Frankfurt/Main	~ 2
Amsterdam-Schiphol	1.5-2.0
Munich Riem	2.5
Manchester	2.4
Orlando/Florida	0.7
Kopenhagen-Kastrup	1.5
Miami/Florida	2.0
Philadelphia	2.1
Lowell (Massachusetts)	1.5
Pittsburgh (Pennsylvania)	1.4
Kansas City	1.6
New York	1.4
South-Florida	1.5
Baltimore-Washington	1.5
Portland	1.3
Toronto	1.4
Stockholm-Arlanda	1.0
Lyon-Satolas	1.5/1.6

Source: Röthlingshofer/Reichhold/Krasser (1988).

In 1994 the Berlin Brandenburg Airport Holding presented several forecasts for the number of passengers travelling from 2004 (first stage of expansion) until 2030 (second stage of expansion) using different margins. Three scenarios reflect the uncertainties in passenger forecasts. From 2010 onwards the distance of a potential airport site to Berlin is incorporated in these estimations.

The employment effects of different airport locations were calculated in the following way. Firstly, the direct effects were determined by using passenger-employment ratios which allow to factor in a productivity increase with rising passenger numbers at the second stage of expansion. The indirect effects were expected to be proportional to the direct ones. We assumed a factor of 1.5 using the mean of the multipliers from the international airports listed above. The estimated catalytic effects were the most insecure (ECAD

2008). In order to reflect this uncertainty properly, a proposed factor ranging between 0.5 and 1.5 was implemented.

The scenario technique exhibits a big fluctuation margin (Table 2). With respect to the first stage of expansion which was planned for the year 2004, the medium scenario amounts to 77.000 jobs in total created through the airport. In contrast the pessimistic scenario yields 52.000 and the optimistic 109.000 jobs. Due to higher capacities, the second stage of expansion is associated with higher employment figures with a bigger range. The average forecast results in 126.000 jobs with a bottom line of 84.000 and an upper bound of 176.000 jobs.

Table 2. Scenarios of employment impacts of a single airport Berlin Brandenburg

Impacts & stage of expansion		1st stage of expansion (2004)	2nd stage of expansion (2030)
Direct impact 1)			
		Passengers in million	
Conservative scenario		17	35
Anticipated scenario		22	45
Optimistic scenario		27	55
		Employees	
Conservative scenario		17,000	28,000
Anticipated scenario		22,000	36,000
Optimistic scenario		27,000	44,000
Indirect impacts			
(estimated factor 1.5)		Employees	
Conservative scenario		26,000	42,000
Anticipated scenario		33,000	54,000
Optimistic scenario		41,000	66,000
Induced impacts			
(estimated factor 0.5 or 1.5)		Employees	
Factor 0.5	Conservative scenario	9,000	14,000
	Anticipated scenario	11,000	18,000
	Optimistic scenario	14,000	22,000
Factor 1.5	Conservative scenario	26,000	42,000
	Anticipated scenario	33,000	54,000
	Optimistic scenario	41,000	66,000

1rst stage of expansion about 1,000 jobs per one million passengers. 2nd stage of expansion about 800 jobs per one million passengers. Source: Bogai/Wiethölter (1994).

Table 3. Scenarios of employment effects depending on potential locations of the airport Berlin Brandenburg

Airport sites & impacts		1rst stage of expansion (2004)1)	2nd stage of expansion (2030)2)
Schönefeld Süd			
Passengers in million		22	45
Employees	direct impact	22,000	36,000
(estimated factor 1.5)	indirect impact	33,000	54,000
(estimated factor 1.5)	induced impact	33,000	54,000
	Total	88,000	144,000
Sperenberg			
Passengers in million		22	41
Employees	direct impact	22,000	33,000
(estimated factor 1.5)	indirect impact	33,000	50,000
(estimated factor 1.0)	induced impact	22,000	33,000
	Total	77,000	116,000
Jüterborg Ost			
Ppassengers in million		22	39
Employees	direct impact	22,000	31,000
(estimated factor 1.5)	indirect impact	33,000	47,000
(estimated factor 0.5)	induced impact	11,000	16,000
	Total	66,000	94,000

1) Direct impact of 1rst stage of expansion: about 1,000 employees per one million passengers.
2) Direct impact of 2nd stage of expansion: about 800 employees per one million passengers.

Source: Bogai/Wiethölter (1994).

This technique was also used to assess the employment effects of the alternative locations for the Berlin airport. The proximity to Berlin determined different multipliers ranging from 0.5 (Jüterbog), 1 (Sperenberg) and 1.5 (Schönefeld) which imply a positive relationship between the number of passengers and the distance to Berlin as another crucial assumption at the second stage of expansion. The alternative passenger forecasts for the three sites at the second stage of expansion were set by the airport holding.

Table 3 shows the results from the IAB analysis. In the first stage of expansion the medium scenario of 22 million passengers annually was set as most likely. According to the estimation, the employment effects of the single airport were the highest in the case of the Schönefeld site. Due to its remote location which reduced the indirect employment effects on the surrounding area, the impact was expected to be approximately one quarter lower in Jüterbog. In the second stage of expansion the differences in the expected passenger traffic become more important as it increases the estimated employment gap. In 2030 only two thirds of the jobs created at Schönefeld would be generated at the Jüterbog site. For labor market and regional policy reasons, the locations in further distance from Berlin should be preferred. It turned out that the international airport would the most beneficial to Jüterbog because of the weak economic situation in this area. Additionally environmental impacts affect quite lower figures of population.

In the inquiry of the House of Representatives Berlin (2016) our conclusion is requoted: "The analysis carried out so far shows that, from an employment policy perspective, the Schönefeld location would be preferable to a large airport BBI. This is due to the higher number of passengers expected there and the stronger economic environment in the region. [...] From a labor market perspective we assess the ranking of the locations exactly in the opposite way. The agglomeration area of Berlin wherein Schönefeld is located all in all probably gain from the suburban migration of the economic activities, while the economic alternatives in the structural disadvantaged Jüterbog district are insecure. From labor market and regional perspective the opportunities offered by the airport location in the agricultural belt of Brandenburg unambiguously are better, since otherwise a persistently high unemployment and an accelerated economic downturn are to be expected" (House of Representatives Berlin 2016: 79).

All in all the early framework – scenarios based on a few multipliers - is with regard to many aspects rather imprecise and can hence only be seen as a rule of thumb assessment. At that time this method was state of the art. The pure suppositions about the divergent factors related to the employment impacts in the different locations had big effects on calculation. That leads to an overestimation of the secondary employment effects and the differences between the alternative locations. Additionally, the poor economic circumstances of the Berlin Brandenburg area compared to other airport regions in Germany remained unrecognized.

3. AIR TRANSPORT SERVICES AND EMPLOYMENT: IMPACT CHANNELS

At the outset of our second study some remarks on the theoretical relationship between airport infrastructure and resulting employment effects are necessary (cf. Bogai/Wesling 2013). Basically, an airport can influence regional economic development in two ways. On one side the demand of an airport and the intermediate inputs associated with it and Keynesian circular loops. Those effects are subdivided into direct, indirect and induced impacts. On the other side an enhanced supply of capable infrastructure fosters productivity increases in the private sector. This influence is called catalytic effect of airport infrastructure.

The usual description differentiates between direct employment-effects through the airport itself, indirect employment effects due to intermediate goods and services and induced employment effect caused by further demand from aggregate income of the direct and indirect employed that increases demand and employment (ACI 2004; Prognos 2008; InterVistas 2015).

In contrast to the direct effects which per definition arise at the airport site, the indirect and induced effects are dependent of the economic conditions and locations of the supply chain. They could arise far away from the airport region. Due to distinct regional economic conditions, varying effects are feasible. Consequently, the secondary employment effects may arise outside the airport region.

On the one hand, better air connectivity stimulates tourism flows. The rising number of incoming tourists pushes demand in the tourism sector. On the other hand outgoing tourism may also be forced. Consequently, purchasing power may flow out from the airport region (Cooper/Smith 2005: 23-28). The latter is very unlikely for the city of Berlin as it frequently ranks among the most attractive metropolises in Europe. The balance of tourism flows and expenditures (inbound – outbound) turns out in favor of the Berlin area where the number of incoming tourists always exceeds the amount of visitors from the previous years.

Airports also ambiguously affect the retail sector. On one side the potential delivery area enlarges, but on the other side the number of potential competitors increases as well. This might diminish the number of firms in the airport area by eliminating the least productive enterprises. The better long distance accessibility improves economies of time and enables just in time delivery of consumer and producer goods. The long haul accessibility is an important location factor for world cities.

The airport infrastructure augments the supply-side of a local economy and affects economies of scale, firm location decision and technical efficiency for commercial users (firms, public institutions). These impacts boost the long term effects on productivity and growth of the airport region. The catalytic impacts operate through two channels. On the one hand an airport can be seen as a further input factor besides labor and capital that has productive outcomes and on the other hand airport services can augment the efficiency and input of other factors of production. In the long run competitive pressure through market expansion causes accelerated structural changes and higher efficiency of firms. The expansion of sales markets could reduce marginal costs and increase economies of scale. Furthermore, efficiency gains are expectable because of reduced transport time.

Another argument refers to the enhancement of labor productivity arising from faster job placement through increased labor supply or higher working time because of reduced travel time. Productivity impacts affect employment contingent on market conditions. In the case of constant output the substitution through more productive labor dominates and employment declines. If price elasticity of demand is sufficiently high, production and employment increase. The region's growing appeal due to the airport triggers more investment of local and new firms which causes accelerating production and employment.

4. PROCEDURE TO IDENTIFY AIRPORT RELATED OCCUPATIONS

After a brief discussion of the impact of airports on employment theoretically we develop an idiosyncratic approach in order to estimate occupational employment effects of major airports. We argue that there are plausible demand and supply side arguments that give evidence for positive employment impacts of the Berlin Brandenburg airport as well as for other regions with airports irrespective of their precise number. The aim given by the politicians was finding branches and occupations that would benefit from the airport and where those are located in the region of Berlin and Brandenburg. For the purpose of infrastructure planning and economic advancement in Brandenburg it is decisive to isolate affected areas. We argue that some occupations are more likely to be found close to airports because they are closely related to its demanded/supplied goods and services. Therefore, a comparison of the occupational structure in areas with major airports should help to identify them. The sensitivity of air transport affine occupations according to changes in aviation industry as a whole is also taken into account here.

According to the classical distinction in the literature we start with direct employment effects, i.e., occupations at the airport site (category I). The indirect effects include occupations in the air transport affine branches that are determined by linking air transport affine branches and main occupations (category II). For reasons of statistical identification (cross matching branches and occupations) direct and indirect employment effects are connected in the empirical results. Finally, a so called overall (gross) employment effect in airport regions (category III) needs to be identified i.e., the geographical concentration of air transport affine occupations. This is done by identifying occupations that are highly concentrated in airport regions. This study is not aimed at dealing with the causality relationship between agglomerations and air transport. The empirical identification can be considered as a funnel-method that is most precise in the direct employment and only tentative in detecting catalytic supply side effects of the airport infrastructure (Figure 1).

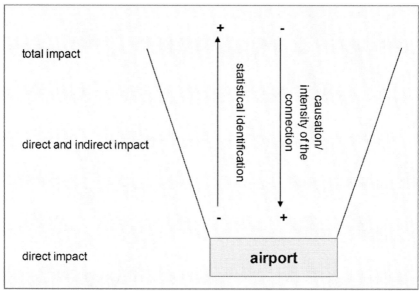

Source: Bogai/Wesling (2010).

Figure 1. Capture of airport affine occupations.

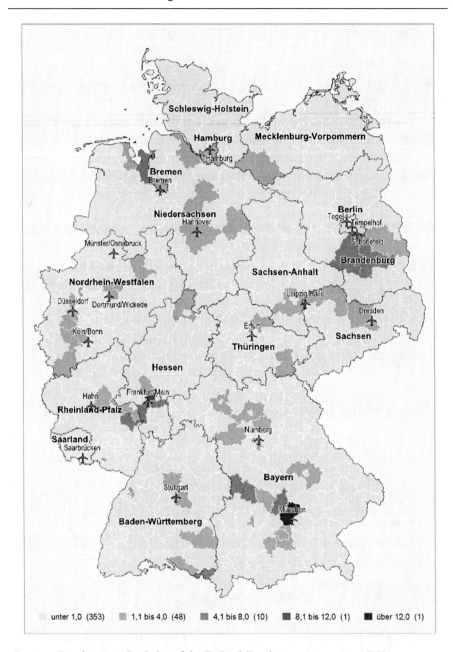

Sources: Employment Statistics of the Federal Employment Agency; ADV; own calculation.

Figure 2. Category II occupations in German districts (share in percent).

The occupations directly connected to the airport (category I) were identified by looking at labor mobility caused by the relocation of the Munich airport from Munich Riem (MUC I) to Munich Freising (MUC II) in 1992. A significant increase of employees commuting from the city district of Munich (former airport location) to the district Freising (new airport location) was identified in the aftermath of this relocation. Those occupations showing an increase in commuter figures between 1990 and 1995 above average are declared as category I occupations (Appendix A).

Category II occupations in our definition are those that are indirectly linked to aviation via manufacturing chains. In order to identify them we heuristically look for air transport affine industries in a first step. Because our main interest is addressed to occupations (and not industries), in a second step the occupations of all German employees in those selected industries were identified. Those occupations which cover more than 0.5 per cent of overall employment in the selected industries were declared as category II occupations. Employees affected by direct and indirect impacts of an airport therefore have - in our definition – to work in one of the 7 air transport affine industries and furthermore in one of the occupations that are important in those industries (Appendix B). To check the validity of this procedure the employment share in category II occupations was calculated for every German district. Figure 2 proofs that this rather naive calculation gives nonetheless quite plausible results.

In almost all districts close to major airports a high degree of category II occupations was found. A remarkable case is the district Wesermarsch in the north of Bremen which exhibits a share of 7.8 per cent of category II employment. Only in three other districts the share of employees related to this category is higher in Germany. The district of Wesermarsch hosts suppliers of aircraft parts and is therefore a relevant site for air transport affine employment although it is not located in the neighborhood of a major German airport.[2]

The comparison of the occupational structure in regions with major airports allows the identification of category III occupations. The selection included the Berlin Airport system (BER), Frankfurt/Main (FRA), Munich (MUC) and Cologne/Bonn (CGN). FRA and MUC are the biggest and most important German airports. Almost halve of the German passenger traffic is processed by these airports. FRA and MUC are also the most important international hubs in Germany. The airport Cologne/Bonn is chosen because –

---

[2] Cf. http://www.premium-aerotec.com.

like the Berlin airport system – it is dominated by the low-cost-carrier segment. Using the equations for each occupation a localization quotient (lq) is determined. This quotient is compared to the federal state (Bundesland) in which the labor market region is located. All occupations whose localization ratio is higher than the Bundesland average in all airport regions, are determined as air transport affine.

$$\frac{\left(\dfrac{SVB_i^{LMR}}{\sum\limits_{i=1}^{336} SVB_i^{LMR}} \right)}{\left(\dfrac{SVB_i^{BRD}}{\sum\limits_{i=1}^{336} SVB_i^{BRD}} \right)} > \frac{\left(\dfrac{SVB_i^{BuLa}}{\sum\limits_{i=1}^{336} SVB_i^{BuLa}} \right)}{\left(\dfrac{SVB_i^{BRD}}{\sum\limits_{i=1}^{336} SVB_i^{BRD}} \right)}$$

Legend:
SVB: Employees covered by social insurance.
i: occupation (i = 1…336).
LMR: labor market region.
BuLa: Federal State in Germany.
BRD: Federal Republic of Germany.

In total 41 occupations fulfill this requirement (Appendix C). Of course the overall effect can be attributed to a mixture of factors like agglomeration forces that are important for major airports and the specialization of economic activities that are connected to long haul accessibility.

Labor market regions of the four airport districts are established by commuter relations (Eckey/Kosfeld/Türck 2006). The total number of employees varies between 1 million in the Köln/Bonn labor market region and 1.3 million in the Berlin labor market region. Incidentally the numbers of employees in category III occupations are approximately similar in three labor market regions with a small deviation for Cologne/Bonn. This fact has the advantage of allowing for direct comparison of the absolute numbers of category III occupations (Appendix B and C).

Table 5. Category III occupations in four German airport regions 2007

	No. of employees (total)	No. of employees (airport affine)	Proportion
Germany	26,854,566	7,636,646	28.4%
LMR Berlin*	1,311,341	430,231	32.8%
LMR Frankfurt/Main	1,084,455	470,771	43.4%
LMR Cologne/Bonn	1,021,447	365,579	35.8%
LMR Munich	1,199,199	479,436	40.0%

* The definition of the labor market region departs from the original notation (Eckey/Kosfeld/Türck 2006) to bring out the belonging of the districts of Brandenburg to the analyzed region.
Source: Employment Statistics of the Federal Employment agency; own calculations.

Table 5 shows a summary of exclusively category III occupations. At first it is found that category III occupations are much more evenly distributed between the regions than category I or category II occupations.[3] The biggest difference exists for office employees (Appendix C). Its high proportion in the capital region (25 per cent) is due to a proliferating public administration.[4] In contrast this proportion amounts only for 14.0 per cent of employees in the agglomeration of Munich. As distinct from the labor market region Munich (17.0 per cent) only 8 per cent of employees in the Berlin-Brandenburg region work in the manufacturing sector.

The employment structure in airport regions reflects to a large extend regional specialization patterns that emerged over a long period of time. An example for regional specialization exhibits the Frankfurt/Main region with its high proportion of bank specialists (13 percent compared to 4.7 percent in Berlin). The lack of economic strength in the capital region is reflected by low shares of business related services with a high degree of knowledge requirements such as consultants, life, property insurance specialists and IT specialists. Two forces were found that might push a catch up for the Berlin Brandenburg region. The dynamic expansion of production and employment since 2005 and better air transport connectivity can jointly boost growth in the services sector. Of course better air connectivity itself without interaction with other sectors does not boost the regional economy. As a necessary condition the economically driven expansion could be enforced by better international air transport services. Especially artists and media specialists considering for example movie industry in Potsdam-Babelsberg and the various film studios in Berlin directly influence the economy and offer growth potential.

---

[3] This is partly caused by different demarcations of airport regions.
[4] Sector L „Public administration, defense, social insurance"(Economic sector classification WZ 2003).

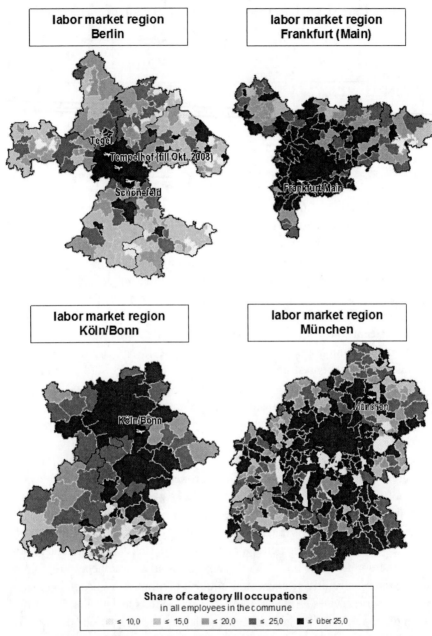

Sources: Employment Statistics of the Federal Employment Agency; own calculations.

Figure 3. Category III occupations in four labor markets regions.

Figure 3 shows the dispersion of category III occupations in the four labor market regions. In the Berlin Brandenburg area these jobs are located in Berlin and in the Brandenburg districts in the south of the capital. In the agglomeration of Frankfurt category III occupations concentrate along the Rhine-Main axis. In the labor market region Cologne-Bonn there are two outstanding areas in the north and south of the airport. The most even distribution of those jobs was found in the Munich labor market region. Overall, the spatial structure of air transport affine jobs is characterized by agglomeration forces and the influence of tourism sites (in the southern regions of Bavaria).

5. SCENARIOS ABOUT THE OCCUPATION-SPECIFIC EMPLOYMENT IMPACT OF THE AIRPORT BERLIN-BRANDENBURG

In this section, the employment trend in airport regions is examined comparatively. The growth rate of category III occupations in the Berlin Brandenburg region was quite different from the overall trend. Between 1995 and 2007 this employment segment grew at an average annual rate of 0.6 per cent compared to an overall decrease of 1 per cent in total employment. In the labor market regions Cologne/Bonn and Frankfurt the growth rate of category III occupations was 2.5 times higher. With an annual growth rate of approximately 2 per cent, the district around Munich which contributes to the core of Bavarian growth, realized the most dynamic development.

**Table 6. Employment of category III occupations
in four LMR 1995 until 2007**

	Growth 1995–2007		Employment share	
	Development	Ø p. a.	1995	2007
LMR Berlin-Brandenburg	6.8%	0.6%	27.7%	32.8%
LMR Frankfurt/Main	19.3%	1.5%	37.1%	43.4%
LMR Cologne/Bonn	19.6%	1.5%	30.5%	35.8%
LMR Munich	25.2%	1.9%	35.1%	40.0%

Data: Employees covered by social security at June 30th.
Sources: Employment Statistics of the Federal Employment Agency; own calculations.

**Table 7. Growth scenarios of category III occupations in
Berlin-Brandenburg**

	2007	2008*	2009*	2010*	2011*	2012*	Difference 2007–2012
Conservative scenario (0.6% growth p. a.)	430,231	432,602	434,986	437,383	439,794	442,218	11,987
Anticipated scenario (1.5% growth p. a.)	430,231	436,608	443,079	449,646	456,310	463,073	32,842
Optimistic scenario (1.9% growth p. a.)	430,231	438,361	446,644	455,084	463,684	472,446	42,215

* Scenario: projection with current rate of growth.
Data: Employees covered by social security at June 30th.
Sources: Employment Statistics of the Federal Employment Agency; own calculations.

In the medium-term perspective the employment share of category III occupations in the labor market region Berlin rose from one quarter in 1995 to a third in 2007. Taking the dynamic expansions in other German regions into account a linear prolongation of the trend in category III occupations seems a reasonable basis for different scenarios. A first conservative scenario reflects the past trend in the Berlin Brandenburg area (0.6 per cent p. a.). The medium and upper scenarios imply long term average growth rates realized in the labor market regions Frankfurt/Main, Cologne/Bonn (1.5 per cent p. a.) and Munich (1.9 per cent p. a.) respectively.

These scenarios do not exhibit causal relationships between delivering air transport services and employment growth. The calculations give an impression on how different growth rates affect the employment figures which reach the number of 40,000 jobs in Berlin Brandenburg in the top scenario. This magnitude coincides with the values calculated by Baum et al. (2005). In this estimation the top result would be realized if employment in Berlin and Brandenburg expands as fast as in the economically powerful labor market region Munich, which is a challenging benchmark for the region.

CONCLUSION

This paper shows the application of scenario technique to calculate employment effects related to a major airport project. The two pragmatic approaches were applied at two stages of the planning procedure of the New Berlin Brandenburg airport "Willy Brandt." The first was was applied to alternative sites of the new single airport in the early planning stage, the second one to assess possible regional and occupational employment effects of the completed airport. The first method represents the state of art during the 1980's. It was calculated that Schönefeld, the site finally chosen, would generate the highest effects on employment because of its short distance to the metropolis of Berlin and its stimulating effects on economic growth in the surrounding area. But for regional policy and environmental reasons the location of the airport in the more distant Brandenburg areas would have been more favorable.

The second assessment approach of employment impacts was performed three years ago prior to the expected opening date of the airport in 2011. Our mission was to find out benefiting industries, occupations and regions in Berlin and Brandenburg. In contrast to the usual quantification framework of magnitudes the study concentrates on structural changes in employment.

The procedure uses the employment statistics that contains 336 occupations and which is able to map the regional development of air transport related employment in 402 German districts. The employment figures are differentiated according to jobs that are directly located at the airport site, employment effects directly and indirectly in the aerospace industry and in related branches. In order to determine a rough indicator for catalytic effects of major airports, a localization ratio of air transport affine occupations was calculated for the main German airport regions.

The results give evidence for direct and indirect employment effects outside the airport site itself in Berlin and for regional effects in the southern districts of Berlin, Dahme-Spreewald, Teltow-Fläming and the city of Potsdam. Most jobs are expected to be related to medium qualified occupations in the tourism sector. The aircraft related industry located in the district Dahme-Spreewald is supposed to stimulate the creation of technical occupations in Brandenburg. The employment impulses are focused notably to male high qualified workers. Separate calculations on community level also confirm employment growth in the local communities surrounding the airport site (Bogai/Wesling 2010) where regional planning is projecting economic and infrastructure developments (Mack 2011).

The most difficult forecast refers to occupations that benefit from better airport infrastructure via catalytic effects. Those impacts are found especially for service occupations with university degree like consultants and managers. The analysis reveals that the trend in the Berlin airport region lags behind other agglomerations in the period investigated. However, the New Berlin international airport would foster the process of catching up that effectively started after 2007. In this process a modern operating airport would give remarkable additional impulses. The airport Tegel offers only a few long distance connections and is strained with overuse. After all, the delay of opening the new airport is likely to irreversibly reduce the positive employment effects that were estimated, because important players established their networks of long haul connections in other regions like Asia or in the Middle East region (Alberts et al. 2009).

Appendix A. Category I occupations

Code	Description of occupation
912	Waiters, Stewards
702	Tourism specialists
726	Air transport occupations
744	Stores, transport workers
933	Household cleaners
701	Forwarding business dealers
411	Cooks
531	Assistants (no further specification)
283	Aircraft mechanics
601	Mechanical, motor engineers
792	Watchmen, custodians
607	Other engineers

Source: Employment Statistics of the Federal Employment Agency; own composition.

Appendix B. Category II industries and occupations

Code	Description
Air transport affine industries	
3530	Manufacture of air and spacecraft and related machinery
6210	Scheduled air services
6220	Nonscheduled air transport
6311	Freight handling
6312	Storage
6323	Supporting and auxiliary services of air transport
6330	Travel agencies and other operators
Air transport affine occupations	
781	Office specialists
702	Tourism specialists
744	Stores, transport workers

Code	Description
Air transport affine occupations	
912	Waiters stewards
726	Air transport occupations
714	Motor vehicle drivers
283	Aircraft mechanics
741	Warehouse managers, warehousemen
601	Mechanical, motor engineers
522	Packagers, goods receivers, despatchers
774	Data processing specialists
701	Forwarding business dealers
751	Entrepreneurs, managing directors, divisional managers
628	Other technicians
261	Sheet metal workers
607	Other engineers
681	Wholesale and retail trade buyers, buyers
621	Mechanical engineering technicians
285	Other mechanics
521	Goods examiners, sorters,
742	Transportation equipment drivers
311	Electrical fitters, mechanics
981	Interns (no occupational specification)
602	Electrical engineers
772	Accountants
782	Stenographers, shorthand-typists, typists
682	Salespersons
151	Plastics processors
752	Management consultants, organizers
784	Office auxiliary workers

Source: Employment Statistics of the Federal Employment Agency; own composition.

Appendix C. Category III occupations

Labor market region	BER	FRA	CGN	MUC
283 Aircraft mechanics	965	2,227	667	1,389
286 Watch-, clockmakers	106	124	128	161
312 Telecommunications mechanics, craftsmen	3,346	1,821	1,582	1,716
611 Chemists, chemical engineers	1,656	3,069	2,281	2,082
626 Chemistry, physics technicians	1,094	1,434	1,032	2,443
634 Photo laboratory assistants	838	462	518	1,231
683 Publishing house dealers, booksellers	1,640	1,187	1,621	2,059
687 Commercial agents, travelers	7,929	10,190	7,135	13,489
691 Bank specialists	20,378	61,420	21,329	36,613
694 Life, property insurance specialists	7,122	9,905	17,814	21,980
702 Tourism specialists	5,462	7,792	3,371	6,186
703 Publicity occupations	7,427	7,017	4,901	8,584
704 Brokers, property managers	1,369	782	551	870
706 Cash collectors, cashiers, ticket sellers, inspectors	1,387	645	922	563

Appendix C. (Continued)

Labor market region	BER	FRA	CGN	MUC
713 Other traffic controllers, conductors	947	504	1,009	958
726 Air transport occupations	2,938	8,289	1,419	3,063
732 Postal deliverers	6,734	4,985	4,861	5,208
751 Entrepreneurs, managing directors, divisional managers	20,234	20,955	17,513	24,685
752 Management consultants, organizers	6,633	11,589	5,852	15,932
753 Chartered accountants, tax advisers	6,996	9,776	6,675	9,288
763 Association leaders, officials	1,529	1,206	854	823
772 Accountants	10,896	8,747	8,806	11,085
774 Data processing specialists	26,711	35,750	25,950	47,446
781 Office specialists	197,115	189,377	164,003	179,466
783 Data typists	1,693	1,607	1,725	1,928
784 Office auxiliary workers	10,916	8,830	10,437	10,453
792 Watchmen, custodians	13,326	10,538	6,001	5,816
813 Legal representatives, advisors	3,869	3,969	2,484	4,333
821 Journalists	5,511	3,680	5,353	7,109
822 Interpreters, translators	637	422	581	649
823 Librarians, archivists, museum specialists	4,440	1,783	2,288	2,606
833 Visual, commercial artists	2,469	1,687	2,083	3,481
835 Artistic and assisting occupations (stage, video and audio)	3,778	1,039	3,260	3,890
836 Interior, exhibition designers, window dressers	687	646	711	876
837 Photographers	780	376	797	823
871 University teachers, lecturers at higher technical schools and academies	6,854	2,449	7,013	2,973
881 Economic and social scientists, statisticians	4,339	4,778	4,156	7,285
911 Restaurant, inn, bar keepers, hotel proprietors, catering trade dealers	6,178	4,576	3,974	6,103
912 Waiters, stewards	17,956	21,122	9,710	17,323
936 Vehicle cleaners, servicers	1,302	1,132	1,267	1,738
982 Interns (no occupational specification)	4,044	2,884	2,945	4,730

Explanation: BER - LMR Berlin; FRA - LMR Frankfurt/Main; CGN - LMR Cologne/Bonn; MUC - LMR Munich.

Source: Employment Statistics of the Federal Employment Agency; own calculations.

REFERENCES

Abgeordnetenhaus von Berlin (2016): Bericht des 1. Untersuchungsausschusses des Abgeordnetenhauses von Berlin – 17. Wahlperiode – zur Aufklärung der Ursachen, Konsequenzen und Verantwortung für die Kosten-und Terminüberschreitungen des im Bau befindlichen Flughafens Berlin Brandenburg Willy Brandt (BER), Berlin, den 14. Juni 2016 [Berlin House of Representatives (2016): Report of the first committee of inquiry of the Berlin House of Representatives - 17th electoral term - to elucidate the causes, consequences and responsibility for the costs and deadlines excesses of the Berlin Brandenburg Airport Willy Brandt (BER) under construction, Berlin, 14th June, 2016]

ACI Europe - Airport Council International, York Aviation (2004): The social and economic impact of airports in Europe, Brussels.

ADV - Arbeitsgemeinschaft deutscher Verkehrsflughäfen (verschiedene Jahrgänge): ADV- Monatsstatistik, Stuttgart/Berlin. [German Airports Association (various years): ADV Monthly Statistics].

Alberts, H. C.; Bowen, J. T.; Cidell, J. L. (2009): Missed Opportunities: The Restructuring of Berlin's Airport System and the City's Position in International Airline Networks. In: *Regional Studies: The Journal of the Regional Studies Association*, 43, 739-758 (20).

Arthur D. Little; German Institute of Economic Research (1993): Economic effects of alternative locations of a single Berlin airport, Berlin.

Baum, H., Schneider, J., Esser, K.; Kurte, J. (2005): Wirtschaftliche Effekte des Airports Berlin Brandenburg International BBI. Im Auftrag der Flughafen Berlin Schönefeld GmbH; Institut für Verkehrswissenschaft Universität Köln und KE-Consult Wirtschafts- und Verkehrsberatung, Köln, [Economic Effects of the Airport Berlin Brandenburg International BBI. Mission of Airport Berlin Schönefeld Ltd.; Institute of Transport Science University of Cologne and KE-Consult Economic and Transport Consulting, Cologne].

Berlin Brandenburg Airport Holding (1993): Results of location search. Summary of surveys, Berlin.

Berlin Brandenburg Airport Holding (1994): Forecasts of passengers 2004, 2030, Berlin.

Blien, U., Hirschenauer, F. (1994): Die Entwicklung regionaler Disparitäten in Ostdeutschland. In: *Mitteilungen aus der Arbeitsmarkt- und Berufsforschung*, 27, 323-337 [The development of regional disparities in Eastern Germany. In: *Jounal for Labor Market Research*].

Bogai, D., Wiethölter, D. (1994): Employment aspects of the three alternative locations for the single airport Berlin Brandenburg. Unpublished manuscript, Berlin.

Bogai, D., Wesling, M. (2010): Großflughafen Berlin Brandenburg. Analyse airportaffiner Beschäftigungspotenziale in Berlin und Brandenburg; Institut für Arbeitsmarkt- und Berufsforschung; IAB-Regional Berlin-Brandenburg No. 02/2010. [Major Airport Berlin Brandenburg. Analysis

of the air traffic related employment potential in Berlin and Brandenburg;
Institute for Employment Research].

Bogai, D., Wesling, M. (2013): The economic effects of air transportation. In:
M. Zajac & R. Nowaczek (Eds), Airports and the automotive industry.
Security issues, economic efficiency and environmental impact,
(Transportation Infrastructure - Roads, Highways, Bridges, Airports and
Mass Transit), Hauppauge: Nova Science Publ., 97-124.

Cooper, A., Smith, P. (2005): The Economic Catalytic Effects of Air Transport
in Europe. EUROCONTROL Experimental Centre, EEC/SEE/2005/004,
Brussels.

GLE (2003): EU Capital Cities study 2003. Brussels/London: Greater London
Enterprise, ALG European Service.

ECAD (2008): Katalytische volks- und regionalwirtschaftliche Effekte des
Luftverkehrs in Deutschland, Darmstadt, [European Center for Aviation
Development: Catalytic political and regional effects of air transport in
Germany].

Eckey, H.-F., Kosfeld, R., Türck, M. (2006): Abgrenzung
deutscher Arbeitsmarktregionen. Universität Kassel, Institut für
Volkswirtschaftslehre, Volkswirtschaftliche Diskussionsbeiträge, Nr.
81/06. [Demarcation of German labor market regions. University of
Kassel, Institute of Economics, Economic Discussion Papers, No. 81/06].

InterVistas Consulting Ltd. (2015): Dublin Airport Economic Impact Study,
Final Report April 2015, URL: http://www.daainternational.ie/wp-
content/uploads/2015/06/Dublin-Airport-Economic-Impact-Study-April-
2015.pdf.

Mach, G. (2011): Planungssituation im Umfeld des neuen Singleairports
der Hauptstadtregion Berlin Brandenburg, in: *Informationen zur
Raumentwicklung*, 16, 47-55 [Planning situation in the surroundings of the
new single airport of the capital region Berlin Brandenburg].

Maier, H. (2008): Planning the airport Berlin Brandenburg international. Use
of statistics and policy making by Berlin and Brandenburg government,
Paper presented to international forum on metropolitan statistics, Bejing
20./21. October 2008.

Ministry of Agriculture Brandenburg, Ministry of City Development Berlin
(1999): Strategy Report Metropolitan Region Berlin-Brandenburg, Berlin.

Prognos (2008): Der Köln Bonn Airport als Wirtschafts- und Standortfaktor.
Die ökonomische Bedeutung von Passagier- und Luftfrachtverkehr,
Düsseldorf. [Cologne Bonn Airport as an economic and location factor.
The economic importance of passenger and freight air transport].

Röthlingshofer, K. C., Reichhold, F., Krasser, G. (1988): Wirtschaftliche und verkehrliche Auswirkungen des Flughafens München II auf sein Umland. ifo-Institut für Wirtschaftsforschung, München. [Economic and transport impact of Munich II airport on its nearby regions. Ifo Institute for Economic Research, Munich].

BIOGRAPHICAL SKETCH

Bogai, Dieter

Affiliation: Institute for Employment Research

Education: MSc in Business Economics, MA in Economics, Ph.D. in Economics Free University of Berlin

Business Address: Friedrichstr. 34, D-10969 Berlin, Germany

Research and Professional Experience: German Council of Economic Experts, Land Employment Agency Berlin Brandenburg of the Federal Employment Agency; Independent Commission on Migration, Federal Ministry of the Interior

Professional Appointments: Senior researcher, Senior Lecturer at the Alice Salomon University Berlin

Publications from the Last 3 Years:

Jost, Oskar; Bogai, Dieter (2016): Foreigners on the labor market in Berlin-Brandenburg. (IAB-Regional, reports and analyzes from the Regional Research Network IAB Berlin-Brandenburg, 01/2016), Nuremberg.

Bogai, Dieter; Carstensen, Jeanette; Seibert, Holger; Wiethölter, Doris; Hell, Stefan; Ludewig, Oliver (2015): A lot of variance: what employees earn in nursing occupations in Germany. Berlin.

Bogai, Dieter (Eds.); Thiele, Günter (Eds.); Wiethölter, Doris (Eds.) (2015): Health care as a regional employment motor. (IAB Library, 355), Bielefeld: Bertelsmann.

Bogai, Dieter; Buch, Tanja; Seibert, Holger (2014): Labor market opportunities for low-skilled workers: Hardly any region offers enough low skilled jobs. (IAB short report, 11/2014), Nuremberg.

Wesling, Mirko; Bogai, Dieter (2014): Return of workers to Brandenburg - An analysis based on the employee history of the IAB. (IAB-Regional, reports and analyzes from the Regional Research Network. IAB Berlin-Brandenburg, 03/2014), Nuremberg.

Bogai, Dieter; Wesling, Mirko (2013): The economic effects of air transportation. In: M. Zajac & R. Nowaczek (Eds.), Airports and the automotive industry. Security issues, economic efficiency and environmental impact, (Transportation Infrastructure - Roads, Highways, Bridges, Airports and Mass Transit), Hauppauge: Nova Science Publ., pp 97-124.

Franziska Hirschenauer

Affiliation: Institute for Employment Research

Education: MSc Geographer, Business Address: Regensburger Str. 100, D---90478 Nuremberg, Germany

Research and Professional Experience: Geographic Institute of the Technical University of Munich; Institute for Employment Research

Professional Appointments: Senior researcher

Publications from the Last 3 Years:

Hirschenauer, Franziska (2015): Demographic change and care work market. In: U. Bettig et al. (Hrsg.), Personnel Development in Care. Analyzes - Challenges - Approaches. Periodical Care Management, Heidelberg: Medhochzwei, p. 1-31.

Hirschenauer, Franziska; Springer, Angelina (2014): Comparison types 2014 * Update of SGB-III typing. (IAB Research Report, 02/2014), Nuremberg.

Hirschenauer, Franziska (2013): New typology of agency areas: Integration success depends on regional circumstances. (IAB short report, 05/2013), Nuremberg.

In: Aviation and Airport Security
Editor: Don Lawrence

ISBN: 978-1-53611-909-1
© 2017 Nova Science Publishers, Inc.

Chapter 3

AIRPORT SECURITY IN THE CZECH REPUBLIC

Lenka Maléřová[1], PhD and Hana Štverková[2], PhD

[1]Department of Civil Protection, Faculty of Safety Engineering, VSB-Technical University of Ostrava, Czech Republic
[2]Department of Business Administration, Faculty of Economics, VSB - Technical University of Ostrava, Ostrava, Czech Republic

ABSTRACT

The aviation transport has gone through dynamic development during last years. The airport security also relates to this turbulence in the aviation industry. The large area with huge accumulation of people at the airports and their surroundings has been the reasons for a targeting to an airport security. This chapter deals with the issue of an airport security in the Czech Republic. The Czech Republic has been an important strategic transport node also with its geographical position such as EU and NATO membership. Within the framework of this chapter, the airport security in the Czech Republic will be analyzed regarding the Safety Risk Management (SRM) setting including the Safety Risk Assessment (SRA) with respect to economic aspects of the issue. The chapter also includes statistical backstage pointing to the topicality of this issue.

INTRODUCTION

After joining the Czech Republic the European Union was significantly extended also the area of an aviation infrastructure. The Czech Republic (thereinafter CR) is a transport hub, based on the strategic geological location, the foreign policy and the membership in NATO and the EU and the Schengen countries. The Czech Republic is a signatory of many international conventions in the field of a civil aviation security (AVSEC) such as the International Civil Aviation Organization (ICAO) [3]. The applicable regulations in the air transport are a consolidated version of Act No. 49/1997 Coll., consolidated version of Decree No. 108/1997 Coll. of the Ministry of Transport and Communications, Ministry of Transport Decree No. 410/2006 Coll. of civil aviation security against illegal acts, Decree No. 466/2006 Coll. of safety flight standard and other [1, 2, 3].

Within the Security strategy of the Czech Republic have been identified security threats of the state, which include asymmetrical threats such as terrorist attacks. Based on the events is it can be assumed, that a possible terrorist attack could be an airport. The airport has been defined as the space with a cumulating of large number of people (up to a million people a day) of different nationalities. The development trend assumes that the passenger numbers will increasingly grow by an average of 6% (ICAO [3]). On basis of this fact it is one of the most important aims of the society to ensure the peoples' security at the airport and its surroundings [1, 2, 3].

The airport means, as amended by Act No. 225/200649/1997 Coll. of civil aviation, the territorially defined and appropriately treated area including the aeronautical buildings and facilities, permanently designated for takeoffs and landings of aircraft and aircraft movements thereto related. An airport can be located on the ground or water. The categorization of airports has been shown in Table 1.

Table 1. The categorization of airports – according to 44/1997 [1]

Graduation	Types of airports	
According to the users and character	Civil airport	Public airport
		Private airport
	Military airport	
According to the equipment, operating conditions and basic determination	Domestic airport	
	International airport	

In the Czech Republic have been in sum 85 airports, where 14 haven been public international airports, 6 private international airports, 56 public domestic airports and 9 private domestic airports. To the general airport network in the Czech Republic belong Vaclav Havel Airport Prague, Leos Janacek Airport Ostrava, Brno - Turany Airport, Karlovy Vary Airport and Pardubice Airport. These airports have fulfilled the conditions for an international airport with an external border of Schengen Area. The methods of an airport security vary in each country; therefore it is the international cooperation very important and also the coordination and standardization of the process among individual states [2, 4].

The operational usability of an airport depends on the airport location, climatological conditions (frequency and intensity of rainfall, fog and weather conditions), an airport equipment (type of runway, hangar and parking options, navigation and technical equipment) and also on the type of provided air services. The attractiveness of an airport depends on the size and density of attraction zone occupancy, whose area depends on the transport connection to residential and industrial places, number of users and additional services (e.g., restaurants, accommodation, entertainment etc.). An airport operation has been based on the authorized aerodrome rules, which determines operation types, services provided, operating and emergency procedures and an airport operator. The airport operator is a physical or legal entity, who is responsible for an observance of aerodrome rules, an operation and maintenance of an airport. The aerodrome rules have been authorized by the Civil Aviation Authority (Czech Republic), which supervises all the civil aviation operation in the Czech Republic [2, 4].

STATISTICS OF AIRPORT ACCIDENTS VERSUS ROAD ACCIDENTS

The probability that a person falls a victim of an aircraft accident is approximately 1: 4 000 000, flying with a prestigious airline. Flying with an airline, which has frequent accidents, the risk is slightly higher but still completely irrelevant. For comparison, the probability that a person dies in a car crash, is about 1: 300. Traffic accidents have been more often with a smaller numbers of injuries or deaths, while the aircraft accidents have been less frequent but with a large number of deaths. Therefore a person often comes to a conclusion that flying has been very dangerous issue but the traffic accidents have been more often as a daily routine [5].

As far as people have been interested how to get safely from the A point to B point, they have been interested on fatality rate convert to a journey kilometer that has been shown in the Table 2. The most important has been the first column, there have been reflected the numbers of victim per billion kilometers (related to one passenger). From the column has been obvious that if someone wants to travel thousand kilometers journey, the best solution has been the choice of an aircraft because the probability of death during the flight has been 1: 20 000 000, while the probability to lose one's life on the same journey on motorcycle has been approximately 1: 9 182 [5].

According to the statistical data (e.g., Global Terrorism Database), it has been indicated that the aircrafts have been the long-term targets of terrorist attacks. Last years, there have been significant increases of terrorist attacks targeting the airports, see the Picture 1 [6].

Based on the Picture 2 it can be pointed that the Czech Republic (Western Europe) has been the destination of potential terrorist attacks. Based on this fact, it has been necessary to ensure the security of airports, employees and passengers located at the airports or immediately near these airports [6].

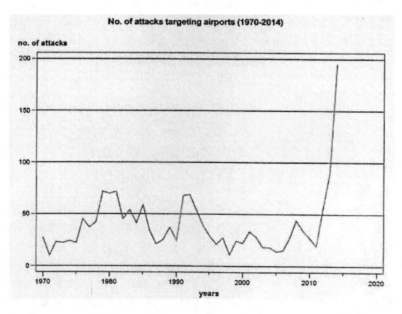

Picture 1. Number of attacks targeting airports in time [6].

Table 2. Number of lose life on the journey [5]

Order	Deaths per billion km	Deaths per billion passengers	Deaths per billion hours
1.	Aircraft (0,05)	Bus (4,3)	Bus (11,1)
2.	Bus (0,4)	Train (20)	Train (30)
3.	Train (0,6)	Truck (20)	Aircraft (30,8)
4.	Truck (1,2)	Car (40)	Ship (50)
5.	Ship (2,6)	On foot (40)	Truck (60)
6.	Car (3,1)	Ship (90)	Car (130)
7.	Bicycle (44,6)	Aircraft (117)	On foot (220)
8.	On foot (54,2)	Bicycle (170)	Bicycle (550)
9.	Motorcycle (108,9)	Motorcycle (1640)	Motorcycle (4840)

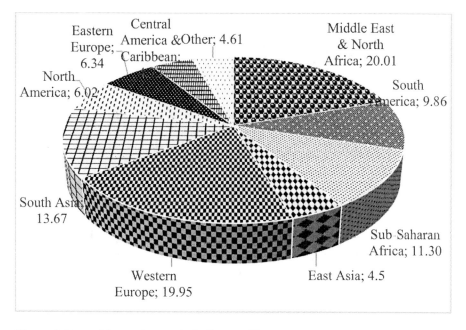

Picture 2. Potential terrorist attacks in Europe [6].

CIVIL AVIATION SECURITY

With the development of the aviation has been developed also its security, therefore, in accordance with crisis plans have been applied different security measures. The security belongs to one of the most important values of every society. Unless the security has not been ensured, the further activities cannot be developed [7].

The term Security in aviation is possible to consider as a situation, where has been no threat to the entity. In this concept, the entities have been primarily the passengers, then the staff in the organizations operating at the airport and all other people in the public part of the airport complex. Even the security of inanimate objects, such as airport buildings, their equipment, wheeled vehicles, luggage and all the aircraft, has been getting on very high level [7, 8, 9].

The most important condition to secure any system has been the initial assumption that no security has been entirely effective. This makes it possible to calculate with a certain risk that an accident will occur and prepare to minimize its consequences [7].

To an active protection of an airport, it has been necessary to completely analyze of the issues, tools, methods and technical solutions needed to prevent possible incidents [10].

The airport building and civil aviation protection has been generally formed a complex of specific security measures and procedures. This complex of measures and procedures fulfills a preventive role and enabling fast response to any illegal act. In designing security measures, it has been necessary to take into account the requirement to maintain the important benefits of air transport, which has been the velocity. This security measures and procedures therefore cannot restrict the velocity and continuity of passengers' clearance and their luggage. The most of the techniques below mentioned have been based on the standards formulated either in Annex 17 to the Convention on International Civil Aviation, or in the Safety Manual of civil aviation organization ICAO (Doc 8973) [3, 10].

The protection of an airport infrastructure does not refer only an activity of state security forces or the airport operator at the airport terminals. Processes that ensure the security of civil aviation against illegal acts begin even far outside of airports. The first security process has been without a doubt the assessment of current threats, security intelligence service and subsequent situational analysis [10].

There has been the reality demonstrated, that the formation of an accident or intentional illegal act occurs precisely because this system has been considered as secure, and therefore nothing can happen. Each technique can break down, as well as the most experienced and best-trained worker can fundamentally fail [10].

RISK AND RISK MANAGEMENT

Risk assessment is the determination of quantitative or qualitative estimating of risk, related to a well-defined situation and a recognized threat. The airport operator, airline operator, air traffic service provider and the service provider (in accordance to § 85a of Act 49/1997 Coll., On Civil Aviation), they have been supposed, during clearance process at the airport, to have an authorized security program of a civil aviation security against illegal acts (hereinafter "program") before starting their operations. The security program has been approved by the Ministry of Transport under the condition that contains measures and procedures to ensure adequate protection for a civil aviation security against illegal acts [11].

The airport security program of the airport provider generally consists of the organization of security protection, preventive measures and emergency planning [11].

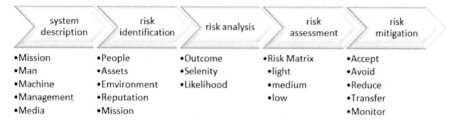

Picture 3. The 5-Step SRM process follows this [11].

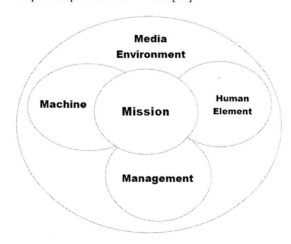

Picture 4. Relationships of the 5M Model [11].

Each airport has an individual risk assessment and evaluation process. Procedures of Safety Risk Management (SRM) have been used for Risk assessment. To evaluate the security risks has been accepted the term Safety risk assessment – SRA, which has been a part of SRM [11].

SRA has been based on the five steps, the system description, the risk identification, the risk analysis, the risk assessment, the risk mitigation; they follow each other continuously, and the steps have been demonstrated on the Picture 3 bellow [11, 12, 13].

First step has been the system description. System in this case may be an airport or its part; this has been depended on the purpose of analysis. The most frequently analyzed components of the system have been the safe movement (e.g., the movement of an aircraft on the airstrip), the activity of individual employees in the system, equipment, coordination, and communication activities, entry conditions for the system (e.g., weather). Media Environment is e.g., airport, terminal, Machine is e.g., equipment, tools, HW, SW, Human Element is e.g., personnel involved, Mission is e.g., functions and objective, Management is e.g., organizational structure, all system is describe at the Picture 4 [11].

The second step has been risk identification. The danger in this context has been the existence of a current or potential condition that can lead to injury, illness or death of people; damage or waste of the system, equipment or property; or environmental damage. The third step has been the risk analysis. This includes decisions, based on the probability and relevance of danger. The fourth step has been the risk assessment. Based on the determination of the probability and relevance of the danger will come to confrontation, whether the risk has been acceptable or unacceptable. The last step has been the risk mitigation. The aim in this case has been the choice of an alternative strategy. This strategy aims to reduce the risk, based on the analysis and risk assessment. An important factor has been the security and also the financial demand of possible mitigation measures. It still remains the essential part, thus the ensuring the peoples' security occurring close to an airport [11].

THREATS TO THE AIRPORT

The ICAO security handbook, there have been described in detail the ways of assessing threats. The security handbook classifies this factors as the presence of extremist groups that may be committed in the attack on the air transport, the incidence of attacks on air travel in the past, internal unrest in the country, or unfavourable economic situation and the volume of air transport and transit of risk flights [3, 10].

Over and over again, in the relation to airports and possible treats to the airport, it has been spoken about so-called asymmetric threats. By this, it means smaller tactical and operational forces against vulnerable points. The purpose of this act is to achieve a disproportionately large effect. Currently, it has been featured six kinds of asymmetric threats - nuclear, chemical and biological weapons, information operations, alternative operational concepts and terrorism [10, 14, 15].

To prevent the creating and minimizing the consequences of the risks, it is necessary to identify the causes connected with sources of risk. The security of protected object, in this case the airport, has been judged in the category of non-military risks. The risks have been following [10, 14, 15]:

- natural risks (floods, overload the roof under the weight of snow, etc.),
- technical risks (spills, damage of technical equipment etc.),
- risks related to illegal acts, where the initiator a human is (criminal activity, terrorism etc.),
- social risks (peoples' assembly, troubles etc.),
- systematic processing (control mechanism and management weaknesses etc.).

The terrorist attacks have not been characterized as a random event, which would be led by some probability distribution. A selection of a destination and a method of an attack have been depending on the knowledge, possibilities and aims of an attacking terrorist organization, therefore it can be certainly nonrandom. Terrorists can for the destructive effects use following facilities [10, 14, 15]:

- booby explosive system,
- flammable products,
- biological and toxicological substances,
- radiological substances,
- chemical substances.

Possible points of attack on the airport from outside can be the airport terminal, garages, close public parking, runway, and airport perimeter. In the buildings, there have been the door, window and other constructions of opened building envelope that can simplify the disallowed entry. Inside the building, there have been the points of contact the bearing element of the construction, energy distribution especially gas), stocks, ventilation systems (danger of gases or chemical substances distribution). In the risk analysis has been played an important role also the Joint Committee for Civil Aviation Security. Its members have been the representatives of the Civil Aviation for Ministry of Transport (Czech Republic), The Ministry of the Interior (Czech Republic), Ministry of Foreign Affairs(Czech Republic), Ministry of Finance (Czech Republic) – the Directorate-General of Customs and the Department of Military Aviation of the Ministry of Defence (Czech Republic). Based on the detected threats, the Joint Committee can formulate the recommendations or according to the information provided, the Ministry of Transport can order the measures for ensuring the security of air transport [1, 2, 3].

At the local level, there have been the most important institutions that have been participate in the risk assessment, airport security committees that have been established by the airport operators at every international airport and other airports, where it has been specified by the Civil Aviation Authority (Czech Republic). The airport security committees have to meet, according to the current regulations, at least four times a year, the Chairman has been the Director or his authorized representative, to other committee members belong representative of the Czech Police, the competent custom office and other companies operating at the airport [1, 2, 3].

On the basis of competencies within the Joint Committee for the security of civil aviation also has been contributed to the risk analysis with the information by the security policy of the Ministry of Interior (Czech Republic) [1, 2, 3].

INTERNAL SURROUNDINGS

Within the ensuring of peoples' security at the airport (the internal surroundings) it is appropriate to complete the airport with closed-circuit televisions (a distinction of monitored objects from relatively constant background and subsequent identification) and with thermic cameras; on the ground of prevention ensuring against a spread of infectious diseases. The security can be empowered by an implementation of a time-limited entering ban for passengers into the area with a security control, e.g., by electrically operated turnstiles and motorized gates. For a peoples' control simplification entering through the service entrance it is possible to use automatic security cabins. According to the biometric parameters (faces and walking) of passengers can be evaluated in cooperation with police of the Czech Republic (peoples' evidence) the identity of dangerous people among the passengers. As a higher level of a security measure, it can be implemented a detection of individual person entering through a revolving door. Gradual rotation allows a closing of people in a detected zone and a sucking of war air flowing around people into the detector for an analyzing of vapor and particles. The hidden detection has been for an airport more convenient, although it decelerates an entering into the departure lounge. Within the security communication strategies is it possible to inform passengers via short leaflets about appropriate behavior in emergency situations. However, this measure has not been accepted by the security management of an airport in relation to negative influence on passengers with an argument that there cannot come any emergency situation at the airport. With thermic cameras can be monitored a situation among the passengers when boarding the aircraft at night using the night vision device, to prevent a unwatched connecting attacker, who passed the perimeter of a landing strip [10].

External Surroundings

In terms of the ensuring of an airport (external surroundings), it is appropriate to implement the perimeter signaling, using the system of sensor cables buried in the ground, that emit a high-frequency electromagnetic field. Connecting the detection zones can be created a protective system of an unlimited length, which generates the detection zone up to 1,5 m high and up to 3 m wide. This system reliably ignores small animals, birds and weather attacks. On the inside of airport perimeter fencing, it is appropriate to build a road for a fast intervention of security forces in case of an airport perimeter attack. The reason has been the reduction of the time interval and also the possibility of the perpetrator detention.

Another recommended security measure has been regular controls of a consistency and functionality of the operating equipment of various companies in the airport terminal for their possible misuse (freezing stands, light advertisement, beverage and gaming machines). For the control of dark spaces, there can be used mobile thermic camera.

Other safety element has been the mechanical and technical protection of access to the airport terminal roof to protect the ventilation and the using of stationary detection systems of CBRNE substances with a stationary collecting places at the air inlets and people entering the airport hall, where have been continuously sucked in the samples to the detectors in the public airport area. In the departure lounge area, it is necessary to keep the overpressure in the direction to the object, and so to prevent an expansion of dangerous substances. It is also advisable to filter the air in parts of the airport hall, which cannot be immediately evacuated.

The terrorist attacks have not been characterized as a random event, which would be led by some probability distribution. A selection of a destination and a method of an attack have been depending on the knowledge, possibilities and aims of an attacking terrorist organization, therefore it can be certainly nonrandom. For those reasons, it is difficult exactly to define the security against these attacks. However, in hold generally the security as introduced at internal and external surroundings [10].

AIRPORT ECONOMICS AND SECURITY

The civil airport has been worked as a commercial company, the company that has been operated its activity for a profit long time. Larger airport activities also bring increased demands on its security.

The possible example has been the enlargement and reconstructions of the Terminal 2 at the Vaclav Havel Airport Prague, its costs have been estimated at 292 million CZK. One of the activity reasons can be the increasing of passenger numbers passing through the airport, and with this fact also the related need to extend the capacity and to modernize the workplace of the central security control. The capacity of security clearance can be increased by a quarter of 2 500 passengers per hour, and ant the same time the new form of a terminal makes a space also for the other possible increasing of capacity to a limit of 3 000 passengers per hour. Therefore, there can come to a modernizing and installation of a completely new automated control lines including the replacement of existing x-ray equipment.

During a seasonality of an aviation have been represented the non-aeronautical activity funds for the yearlong coverage of an airport operation and have been participated in the coverage of security measures. The disadvantage may have been the fact that many airports, based on the market principle, invest into the security measures only what the law imposes and the prevent security ensuring beyond the statutory obligation has not been necessary for airports.

The effort to save in air traffic partly affects the security aviation. In relation to the non-binding and the economic costs of security recommendations, some airport operators do not fulfill these recommendations, arguing with fulfilling of everything what the law orders, and the recommendations have not been binding. [10, 16].

CONCLUSION

The economic development supported by political and economic changes, pointing to the worldwide globalization of goods production, also goes with the globalization of transport infrastructure. With a development of a society and the inclusion of the Czech Republic into the NATO and European Union, together with a development of engineering and trading became the Czech Republic due to its geographic location to the traffic junction connecting East and West.

In the Czech Republic have been in sum 85 airports, where 14 haven been public international airports, 6 private international airports, 56 public domestic airports and 9 private domestic airports. To the general airport network in the Czech Republic belong Vaclav Havel Airport Prague, Leos Janacek Airport Ostrava, Brno - Turany Airport, Karlovy Vary Airport and Pardubice Airport.

The most important aim is to ensure the population security, related to this fact also the security ensuring of civil aviation.

Based on this fact, it is necessary to ensure the airport security on the basis of risk identification. Among the monitored risks, there can be classified natural risks, technical risks, risks related to illegal acts, social risks and system-procedural risks. More and more often, in relation to airports and possible threats has been spoken about so-called asymmetric threats. There can be the smaller tactical and operational forces against the vulnerable areas. Currently have been reported six types of asymmetric threats – nuclear, chemical and biological weapons, informative operations, alternative operational concepts and terrorism.

Within the risk evaluation has been the acceptation of security measures, which can be divided into external (airport surroundings) and internal (airport, terminal) measures. It should be noted that the measures have been closely related to the economics. Greater security can bring greater financial burden for an airport.

In relation to the security, it is necessary to refer to the fact that sometimes one hundred percent of security can lead to a worse disaster, as for example in France, where in March 2015 a German pilot wittingly lead the low-cost airbus Germanwings on the flight from Barcelona to Duesseldorf into the rock of the French Alps; the crew could not get into the cabin of the aircraft [17]. One source has reported that on the basis of security equipment, there was no way to get into the cockpit, the other one has reported that in case of one pilot outside the cabin can get inside in few minutes, if there has been no emergency technical failure. Additionally, pilots generally know the code for opening the door. It has been necessary to consider, if possible security measure cannot harm instead of help within the security.

REFERENCES

[1]   Government of the Czech Republic. Security strategy of the Czech Republic 2015 [online]. Government of the Czech Republic, 2015. 24 pages [quote 2016-04-29]. Available on: http://www.mzv.cz/file/ 1386521/Bezpecnostni_strategie_2015.pdf.

[2]   MINISTRY OF TRANSPORT. Concept of air transport for the period of 2015 - 2020 [online]. Prague: Ministry of Transport, 2015. 89 pages [quote 2016-04-29]. Available on: http://www.mdcr.cz/NR/rdonlyres/ B42FF1D9-2247-4A82-A993-348EB05E1E01/0/Material.pdf.

[3]   ICAO. Forecasts of Scheduled Passenger and Freight Traffic [online]. [quote 2016-04-29]. Available on: http://www.icao.int/sustainability/ pages/eap_fp_forecastmed.aspx.

[4]   KOVERDYNSKÝ, Bohdan. Security of civil aviation: history, organisation, standards, procedures. *Prague: Department of Security Policy of the Ministry of the Interior of the Czech Republic*, 2007. 104 pages.

[5]   Modern Railways, 2000 (DETR Survey), date from 1990 – 2000. [online]. [quote 2016-04-27]. Available on: http://technet.idnes.cz/jak-bezpecne-je-letani-letecke-nehody-statistiky-f64-/tec_technika.aspx?c =A150324_175335_tec_technika_pka.

[6]   Global Terrorism Database [online]. [quote 2016-04-27]. Available on: http://www.start.umd.edu/gtd/.

[7]   WAISOVÁ Š. Safety - Development and changing concept. Plzen: Publishing Ales Cenek, 2005, pp. 7-8.

[8] ZAVILA, O. Fire Protection Systems in the Ilyushin Il-28: The Only Jet Bomber in the Czechoslovak and Czech History. *Advances in Military Technology*, 2015, roč. 10, č. 2, s. 71-79.

[9] POKORNÝ, J. - TOMÁŠKOVÁ, M. - BALAŽIKOVÁ, M. Study of changes for selected fire parameters at activation of devices for smoke and heat removal and at activation of fixed extinguishing device. Praha: MM (Modern Machinery) Science Journal (indexed in Scopus). 2015, s. 764 - 767. ISSN 1803-1269 (Print), ISSN 1805-0476 (On-line). DOI: 10.17973/MMSJ.2015_12_201558.

[10] ŠČUREK, R., ŠVEC, P. *Protecting airports from illegal acts*, 2009, ISBN: 978-80-7385-071-5, 126 s.

[11] ELIAS, Bartholomew. Airport and Aviation Security: U. S. Policy and Strategy in the Age of Global Terrorism. Boca Raton, FL: CRC Press, 2009. 439 pages. ISBN 978-1-4200-7029-3.

[12] ČSN EN 31000:2011Risk management – Principles and guidelines. Prag: Czech Standards Institute, 2008.

[13] ČSN EN 31010:2011. Risk management – Risk assessment techniques. Prag: Czech Standards Institute, 2008.

[14] AVIATION SAFETY REPORTING SYSREM. Request No. 1634, Fulap setting on approach/pandiny ASRS office, Mountain View, Kalifornia, USA. 1989.

[15] NTSB: Safety study: A review of flightcrew-involved, major accidents of U. S. aircarriers, 1978 through 1990 (PB94-917001 NTSB.SS-94/01). Washington DC: National Transportation Safety Board, 1994.

[16] Economy today [online]. [quote 2016-04-27]. Available on: http://ekonomika.idnes.cz/letiste-ceka-rozsireni-za-ctvrt-miliardy-pribude-odbaveni-i-obchodu-11b-/eko-doprava.aspx?c=A160729_150530_eko-doprava_suj. [Enlargement of Airport]

[17] Newes Idnes[online]. [quote 2016-04-27]. Available on: http://zpravy.idnes.cz/germanwings-lubitz-problemy-ve-skole-d8p-/zahranicni.aspx?c=A160830_194524_zahranicni_abakdy na základě bezpečnostního zařízení. [Germanwings pilot]

In: Aviation and Airport Security
Editor: Don Lawrence

ISBN: 978-1-53611-909-1
© 2017 Nova Science Publishers, Inc.

Chapter 4

LISTENING TO THE VOICE OF THE PASSENGERS: AN APPLICATION OF LEAN SIX-SIGMA PRINCIPLES TO AIRPORT CAPACITY MANAGEMENT

Tony Diana[*], PhD

Federal Aviation Administration,
Washington, DC, US

ABSTRACT

This study used the case of ATL to illustrate the links between airport capacity management and passenger satisfaction measured as airlines' on-time performance. The analysis relied on several assumptions. First, airport operators and air traffic control play a significant role in minimizing variations in airport capacity utilization, which may affect airlines' on-time performance and, as a result, passenger satisfaction. Reducing process variability and improving gate-to-gate processes both represent the key principles of a lean sigma approach to flight operations. Second, the implementation of NextGen capabilities and procedures reduced the variability of unutilized airport capacity. A comparison of two samples revealed that the standard deviation of unutilized airport capacity decreased, while the sigma level improved from 2.6 (March to May 2015) to 2.9 (March to May 2016)

---

[*] Corresponding Author: tonydiana@aol.com.

during the core hours of 7:00 to 21:59 (local time). By minimizing the variability of unutilized capacity, airlines reduced gate departures and arrival delays by about two minutes on average compared with airlines' flight plan estimates, while the number of operations and available capacity both increased.

INTRODUCTION

One of the core functions of air traffic control (ATC) is to manage available airport capacity efficiently and effectively. In the case of the U.S. Federal Aviation Administration (FAA), air traffic control (ATC) refers to several levels of traffic management: airport towers, Terminal Radar Approach Control (TRACON) facilities, Air Route Traffic Control Centers (Centers), and the Air Traffic Control System Command Center (ATCSCC). A TRACON usually oversees arrival and departure flows within a radius of 40 nautical miles around an airport, whereas centers control the enroute portion of flights—approximately 100 nautical miles from airports. The ATCSCC manages air traffic flows throughout the National Airspace System (NAS). This article focuses on the tower facility.

Available airport capacity represents the sum of arrival and departure capacity. This article deals with one key measurement in airport capacity management: the percentage of total unutilized airport capacity (also referred in this article as unutilized airport capacity). It is defined as 100 percent minus the ratio of total operations (*observed* arrivals plus departures) to declared airport capacity (*estimated* airport arrival plus departure rates). Every day, the ATCSCC determines airport arrival and departure rates at the largest 77 airports in collaboration with representatives from airport facilities, airlines, weather services, and other key NAS stakeholders. The selection of runway configurations allows ATC to change capacity utilization by adjusting airport arrival and departure rates accordingly. The latter define the optimal number of aircraft that can arrive and depart safely given several factors: airline schedules, arrival and departure demand, weather conditions (ceiling and visibility), wind direction, periods of peak operations, and separation standards,[1] among other major factors.

The queueing theory predicts that, as capacity utilization increases, available runways are less capable of meeting agreed levels of service, which

---

[1] As defined by FAA Order 7110.65 retrieved at https://www.faa.gov/regulations_policies/orders_notices/index.cfm/go/document.information/documentID/1028576.

results in increased wait times, longer lines, and sometimes balking (aircraft go-arounds). Thus, ATC's challenge consists in maintaining an 'optimal' level of capacity to prevent either congestion and delays or unutilized resources. When airport capacity is unutilized for extended periods, an airport stands to lose revenues in the form of landing and gate fees, among others. Airport congestion and delays are likely to increase when airport capacity is close to full utilization, with no slack for unanticipated arrivals and departures. Therefore, airlines will not be able to meet passengers' expectations of on-time gate arrivals and departures. If airlines cannot recover from delays, they may resort to flight cancellations. Although delays may have a negative impact on airport and airline operations, ATC is sometimes compelled to implement ground stop delays or other traffic flow management initiatives (TMI) such as miles- or minutes-in-trail to help an airport recover capacity and manage demand. A key challenge for airlines is to explain to their passengers that delays may be necessary to improve the overall capacity of the NAS. Capacity management, especially at large congested hubs, affects both incoming and outgoing traffic flows or throughputs.

Thus, airport capacity management has some important ramifications for society and beyond the aviation arena in the form of external costs. Congestion and delay generate external costs, not only to airlines in terms of higher fuel burn, carbon emission, and crew costs, but also to passengers in terms of "lost passenger time due to flight delays, cancellations and missed connections, plus expenses such as food and accommodations that are incurred from being away from home for additional time."[2] Based on a 2010 Nextor report, flight delays cost $32.9 billion using 2007 data. While the costs to airlines were estimated at $8.3 billion, passenger costs represented $16.7 billion (Ball et al., 2010).

Airport capacity management plays a significant role in guaranteeing a level of service (on-time arrivals and departures) that meets both airlines and passengers' expectations. Besides operational factors, airport capacity management is also related to the competitive structure of the airline industry, market concentration at specific airports, and advances in ATC technologies deployed at both airports and in the enroute environment. After the Great Recession of 2008, airline consolidation gained pace, especially in the United States where four large air carriers (American, Delta, Southwest, and United)

---

[2] Ann Brody Guy, "Flight delays cost $32.9 billion, passengers foot half the bill", Berkeley News, University of California Berkeley, October 18, 2010 retrieved at http://news.berkeley.edu/2010/10/18/flight_delays.

now account for about 70 percent of the domestic passengers.[3] At the same time, the FAA embarked into a modernization program to transition the ATC from a radar-based to a satellite-based navigation system. The Next Generation Air Transportation System or NextGen capabilities are designed to increase available capacity, especially at large congested airports, and to utilize technologically-advanced flight procedures to improve flight predictability and reduce delays.

In the last ten years, few new runways have been put in service in the United States. This may be due to a variety of factors such as surrounding airport's community resistance, high costs of runway construction, airport operators' constrained budget, and sometimes lack of available space for airport expansion. Runway construction projects may take more than a decade at a cost sometimes exceeding a billion dollars. Despite these challenges, airports as regional economic engines must attract and retain airlines to grow and compete. They need to collaborate, not only with airlines to ensure passenger satisfaction with terminal amenities (available gates, parking facilities, waiting lounges, and concessions), but also with ATC to ensure flights operate on time.

This study uses the case of Atlanta Hartsfield/Jackson International Airport (ATL) to determine how some of lean six-sigma concepts may help ATC, airport and airline operators capture the 'voice of the process' (requirements for 'optimal' available airport capacity) and the 'voice of the passengers' (requirements for on-time arrivals and departures). ATL represents an interesting case for several reasons. First, the dominant air carrier, Delta Air Lines, merged with Northwest Airlines. Secondly, the FAA has introduced some significant capabilities such as wake vortex re-categorization, equivalent lateral spacing operations, time-based flow management, adjacent center metering, among others. Third, despite an increase in operations observed between two samples, airlines managed to reduce gate arrival and departure delays, as well as their overall on-time performance.

In the lean six-sigma approach, no improvement in processes is possible without understanding the voice of the customers and the voice of the process. The voice of the customer is a key input to a quality function deployment (QFD) matrix, which helps management, in a manufacturing environment, proceed through four main phases: (1) customer expectations (functional

---

[3] Source: U.S. Department of Transportation, Bureau of Transportation Statistics, September 2015-August 2016, retrieved at http://www.transtats.bts.gov.

requirements), (2) product design (design characteristics), (3) development (process characteristics), and (4) production (process capability). While a six-sigma approach is mainly a strategy to reduce drastically the number of defects, lean six-sigma is more focused on eliminating waste, streamlining procedures, and improving process speed to meet customers' expectations. Nevertheless, both approaches share the common goal of improving quality.

According to ISO 9000 standards, quality "is the degree to which a set of inherent characteristics fulfill requirements."[4] Crosby (1980) defined quality as conformance to requirements. For Taguchi (1990), quality represents the ability to meet a target with little variation. In our case, a flight meets passengers' expectations if it arrives or departs no later than the times specified in the flight plan. The definition of the U.S. Department of Transportation (USDOT) for delay[5] slightly differs: A flight is counted as "on time" if it operated less than 15 minutes compared with the scheduled time shown in the carriers' Computerized Reservations Systems (CRS). Arrival performance is based on arrival at the gate, while departure performance is based on departure from the gate, both compared with airlines' announced schedule times. While the CRS reflects airlines' commitments to the public, estimated arrival and departure times in the flight plans do not include schedule padding, which is often added to the estimated flight time to reflect potential ground and enroute delays (Wu, 2010).

To understand the challenges related to airport capacity management, this study will examine some key elements in lean six-sigma: the variability and the specification limits of the percent of unutilized airport capacity, as well as airport throughput capability through long-term process performance assessment. A design of experiments (DOE) will help identify the factor(s) that may affect variations in the percentage of unutilized airport capacity.

LITERATURE REVIEW

Few studies in the aviation industry have utilized lean six-sigma principles to evaluate the voice of the passengers. No research has attempted to link airport capacity management with passenger satisfaction measured as on-time

---

[4] International Standards Organization (2015). ISO 9000: 2015. Quality management systems: fundamental and vocabulary, 4th edition. Geneva, Switzerland: ISO.
[5] See Title 14, Chapter II, Subchapter A, Part 234 (14 CFR 234) retrieved at: https://www.law.cornell.edu/cfr/text/14/part-234.

gate performance. Airlines have often resorted to passenger surveys or benchmarking to assess passenger satisfaction and retention.

Cronin and Taylor (1992) studied the relationship between service quality, customer satisfaction, and purchase intentions and investigated how to conceptualize and measure service quality. They tested three questions designed to identify (1) how service quality construct should be measured, (2) how service quality is related to consumer satisfaction, and (3) what customers' purchasing intentions are. The authors advocated performance-based measures of service quality, which, in their view, should be measured as an attitude. Although, on-time performance is critical to quality for passengers, Gilbert and Wong (2003) concluded that passengers were also concerned by safety and security following the events of September 11, 2001. They relied on studies of passenger expectations and airline services in the case of Hong Kong.

Chen (2002) used the example of Chiang Kai Check International Airport (CKS) in Taiwan to apply a quantitative model designed to link performance indicators with benchmarking process. The author tried to evaluate the voice of the passengers in their benchmarking study. The study emphasized the "convenience of transport facilities connecting to the outside", the "interior design and layout," and the "information service of the airport" as key benchmarking items. However, benchmarking did not address the operations side of passenger experience such as tarmac and gate delays, for instance.

Passenger retention is important for airlines. The industry has been a forerunner in introducing programs such as frequent flyers, cabin services, and seating upgrades, among others. Petrick (2004) examined the relationship between satisfaction, perceived value, and quality as predictors of repurchase and word of mouth. In the case of cruise passengers, he concluded that service quality predicted the best passengers' intention to repurchase. Service quality extends beyond passenger terminal amenities, shopping experience at airports, and access. It is also likely to depend on on-time experience. Nowadays, passengers are more willing to tolerate fewer services onboard in exchange for lower fares. However, they are less likely to compromise on on-time performance.

When examining airline service quality from a process perspective, Chen and Chang (2005) determined that passengers had different expectations at different stages of a flight: in-flight versus ground service stages. If the percentage of capacity utilized supports passenger satisfaction through on-time performance, then it is important to determine whether airborne delays and gate arrival delays may influence an airport's capacity utilization. The theory of airport capacity predicts that when demand approaches capacity, then delays are likely to increase. Aircraft are likely to spend more time in a takeoff line, while those arriving may be delayed through TMI (see U.S. Congress, Office of Technology Assessment report, 1984). The capacity of a runway depends on the time it takes for an aircraft to land and move to the taxiway (runway occupancy rates), ceiling and visibility conditions, as well as separation standards, among other significant factors.

Luo (2007) used longitudinal real-world data related to the airline industry to show that consumers' negative voices could influence stock returns. On-line websites have the potential to magnify these negative voices. Therefore, it is important for organizations to invest in improving negative voices. The Bureau of Transportation Statistics (BTS) of the USDOT ranks the major domestic carriers based on on-time performance and lost baggage.

Czermy and Zhang (2011) made an interesting connection between airport capacity, congestion pricing as a capacity management tool, and passenger satisfaction. When airlines do not practice passenger-type-based price discrimination, the authors recommended that airports apply charges to protect passengers with a great relative time value from excessive congestion caused by passengers with a low relative time value. One important assumption in this research is that on-time performance is critical to quality for passengers. However, no assumption is made about passengers' relative time value, which is likely to depend on whether a passenger travels for business or leisure. In terms of policy, peak period pricing, congestion pricing, and slot auction, among other tools, have been advocated to manage arrival and departure demand (see Pels and Verhoef, 2004; Ball et al., 2007).

Alsyouf et al., (2014) used the five phases of the six-sigma approach (define, measure, analyze, improve, and control) to study the process of baggage handling Based on qualitative and quantitative methods, the authors identified four main problems: lack of adequate training, long working shifts, conveyor system breakdown, and falling bags. The six-sigma approach enabled the identification of critical causes and the selection of the best alternatives to solve identified problems. One benefit of their approach was the identification of targets that made it possible for airport operators to evaluate and monitor performance, as well as to ensure continuous improvements in baggage handling.

METHODOLOGY

Assumptions and Hypotheses

Although the USDOT releases monthly statistics on major air carriers' performance,[6] airlines and ATC do not collect and analyze data from passengers' experience after their flights. Therefore, it is important for airlines to evaluate the variability of some selected factors may have an important impact on-time performance. Several reasons make the use of lean six-sigma principles appealing to measure the 'voice of the passengers' and the 'voice of the process'.

First, airlines and ATC cannot determine with certainty the upper and lower specification limits that define 'the voice of the passengers' and the upper and lower control limits that outline the 'voice of the process.' It is difficult for airlines to aggregate and rank passenger's preferences because passengers differ in terms of choice of airlines (preference for low-cost versus legacy carriers), airfares, on-board services, and purpose of travel, among many other factors. Nevertheless, passenger retention may serve as an indicator of how well an airline satisfies its passengers. On-time performance is a factor that airlines often tout in their marketing campaign and corporate communications.

Second, the theory of airport capacity predicts that capacity, delay, and demand are closely related. De Neuville (1976:135) explained the relationship among these variables as follows:

> The performance of a service system is, indeed, sensitive to the pattern of loads especially when they approach its capacity [...] A service facility [...] does not provide equal service at all times; its service rapidly deteriorates as traffic nears capacity. A service facility, can, furthermore, eventually handle more than its immediate capacity by delaying traffic until an opportunity for service exists.

Presumably, if ATC can anticipate the volume of operations more accurately, it may be able to declare arrival and departure rates that would

---

[6] The Airline Service Quality Performance (ASQP) report provides on-time performance, cancellations, and causes of delay for the domestic carriers that account for one percent or more of total domestic scheduled service passenger revenues. These carriers operate within the 48 contiguous states. The U.S. Department of Transportation requires that airlines file information under 14 CFR 234.

minimize airport congestion and delays. Therefore, a closer look at the frequency and magnitude of special cause variations in statistical process control charts may detect specific times when passenger may have been dissatisfied due to higher utilized airport capacity. In an X-bar/S-chart, the dots higher or below the specification limits suggest that airport traffic may have been increased or reduced beyond normal circumstances (special cause).

Third, six-sigma principles can help aviation practitioners identify on-time performance targets. Six sigma relies on data analysis to evaluate short and long-term variability in order to gauge the 'voice of the process' and the 'voice of the passengers'.

Fourth, it is important for ATC, airport and airline operators to understand what is critical to passengers. Kano (1984) presented a two-dimensional model based on achievement (X-axis) and satisfaction (Y-axis) to understand customers' needs and gather the 'voice of the customers.' Kano's model acknowledges that customers have basic, expected, and exciting needs. In the present case, basic needs refer to leaving and departing on time. Passengers expect pilots to do their best to catch up with any delay on the ground and enroute. They are delighted if their flight arrives earlier than scheduled at the gate. Whereas on-time arrivals and departures are 'critical to process' for ATC, airline and airport operators, on-time performance is 'critical to quality' for passengers.

Key Performance Metrics

The metrics in Table 1 pertain to two sampled periods: March to May 2015 and 2016, respectively. Each period covers the core operations hours of 07:00 to 21:59 (local times), for all days of the week. It does not separate operations into instrument versus visual approach conditions—when ceiling and visibility exceed minima at ATL. The March to May period was selected because it does not include peak seasonal traffic and it is less likely to be influenced by convective weather, which may force ATC to implement traffic management initiatives. Traffic Flow Management System (TFMS) was the source of traffic mix percentages computed for all hours of the day. The causes of delay in percentages are based on the total delays reported by the largest domestic carriers to USDOT on a monthly basis. The actual gate arrival and departure times were compared with the time that airlines filed in their flight plans. All data in Table 1 originated from the Aviation System Performance Metrics (ASPM) data warehouse.[7]

While total operations increased 2.24 percent, the total available capacity rose 2.73 percent when comparing both samples. Wake vortex re-categorization or 'wake recat' implemented after June 1, 2015 may explain the increase in the total available capacity. Wake recat allows shorter inter-arrival and departure times between pairs of aircraft.[8]

In the post sample, the declining share of the Boeing 757 in the traffic mix and the increase in large jets (Boeing 737 or Airbus A320) reflect Delta's fleet restructuring. The share of heavy aircraft such as the Boeing 777 or Airbus A330 remained constant at 5 percent. 'Other' includes larger and smaller commuter aircraft. The categories of aircraft depend on their incidence on wake vortex.

During the period of March to May 2016, delays related to air carriers represented a larger share of the total delays reported by the major carriers, while the share of extreme weather and NAS delays declined. Air carrier delays refer to mechanical problems or delays loading baggage or catering, for instance. NAS delays include traffic management initiatives and weather delays due to low ceiling and visibility. Extreme weather refers to events such as heavy snowstorms and thunderstorms, tornadoes, and hurricanes, for instance.

Table 1. Key Performance Metrics at ATL

Variable	March-May 2015	March-May 2016
Operations (Arrivals plus Departures)	202,907	207,469
Percent Capacity Utilized	64.28	63.98
On-Time Gate Departures	84.61	86.98
Total Available Capacity	315,664	324,293
Departure Delay (minutes)	8.03	6.43
On-Time Gate Arrivals	86.95	90.19
Arrival Delay (minutes)	7.93	5.59
Traffic Mix (Percent)		
Heavy	5	5
Boeing 757	11	9
Large Jets	63	66
Other	21	21

---

[7] FAA's performance metrics are available at https://aspm.faa.gov.
[8] Federal Aviation Administration, "NextGen stirs up efficiency in its wake," December 2015, retrieved at: https://www.faa.gov/nextgen/snapshots/stories/?slide=41.

Variable	March-May 2015	March-May 2016
Causes of Delay (percent)		
Air Carriers	37.37	43.07
Weather	4.96	3.73
NAS	21.55	16.26
Security	0.05	0.06
Late Arrivals	36.07	36.88

Statistical Process Control: Checking the Variability of Unutilized Capacity

Figure 1 shows the X-bar (mean)/S-chart (standard deviation) from Minitab®. The chart uses all the data points and, thus, is an accurate indicator of unutilized capacity variation. There were 92 subgroups whose size was 15 hours (from 07:00 to 21:59 local time, when data were collected).

At a 95 percent level, we accept the null hypothesis that the mean unutilized airport capacity did not change significantly ($p = 0.189$). However, we reject that null hypothesis that the standard deviation of unutilized airport capacity did not change from March to May 2016 compared with the pre-sample.

($p < 0.005$). Since the Levene's test determined that $p = 0.000$, we reject the null hypothesis that the variance of unutilized capacity in the pre and post-samples was equal. In fact, it declined 16.8 percent from March to May 2016 compared with March to May 2015. The distance between the upper and lower control limit (UCL and LCL) of the S-chart shows a narrower range of variation in unutilized capacity in the March-to-May-2016 period (u_caputil_2) than in the March-to-May-2015 period (u_caputil_1). A lower standard deviation value implies less variability of the percentage of unutilized airport capacity. The square dots below the lower control limit indicate special causes of unutilized capacity potentially related to ground delay programs and other traffic management initiatives.

The FAA implemented several initiatives at ATL, which may have contributed to improve arrival and departure throughputs and, thus, minimize unutilized capacity. In October 2011, ATC started to use Equivalent Lateral Spacing Operations (ELSO), which enables diverging departures routes. Because less separation between aircraft is required for diverging departure routes, ATC can increase the number of takeoffs at peak times (departure throughputs) and, thus, minimize unutilized departure capacity. In May 2012, ATC integrated the Automated Terminal Proximity Alert (APTA) procedure designed to reduce go-arounds in terminal airspace as well as spacing between aircraft on their final approach to the airport. In June 2015, ATL implemented wake recat, a procedure that makes it possible for ATC to reduce the separation between aircraft and increase throughputs. Using Markov regime-switching regression, Diana (2015) found that periods of high departure throughputs lasted longer than periods of constrained throughputs after the implementation of wake recat.

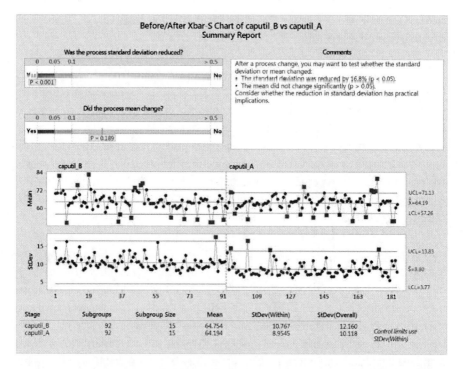

Figure 1. X-Bar and S-Chart Outputs (March-May 2015 as u_caputi_1, March-May 2016 as u_caputi_2).

Process Capability Analysis

Capacity management is a process that starts from gate departure at the origin airport to gate arrival at the destination airport. It also includes airborne time (wheels-off to wheels-on time). Any constraints between those four key flight events (gate-out, wheels-off, wheels-on, and gate-in) may have an impact on unutilized capacity. These constraints include:

- Surface delay due to ramp and taxiway congestion
- Delays at departure, arrival and enroute
- Taxi-in and out delays, and
- Ground stop delays, among others.

Delays do not add any value to the departure or arrival processes and may be construed as a 'waste' of capacity: They prevent traffic from flowing through the key flight events, they generate external costs, and they lead to passenger dissatisfaction. An increase in delays at these four key events may be indicative of bottlenecks. Nevertheless, some delays triggered by ATC may be designed to slow down operations between the four key flight events so that an airport and the NAS may recover from major weather events or lack of available capacity.

Constraints at one of the four key events set the pace of upstream and downstream flows, which eventually affects airport utilization. Based on Goldratt (1990) who developed the theory of constraints, the 'drum' is the departure and arrival throughputs (the rate of hourly departures and arrivals). The 'buffer' regulates traffic flows through the four key events and provides some slack in airport capacity to enable continued operations. The 'rope' controls the traffic flows through the four key events to prevent a surge of delays. For instance, time-based flow management (TBFM) rations aircraft hand-offs to a TRACON and subsequently to an airport based on available capacity in the terminal area and at the airport of destination. Ground delay programs keep aircraft at the gates to prevent delays from increasing and propagating throughout the NAS. ATC can increase miles or minutes in trail to regulate the volume of arrivals and departures. The Center, TRACON, terminal, and tower all create the critical chain which plays an important role in managing delays during the major phases of a flight (Goldratt, 1997).

Airport capacity management also depend on several factors that constrain arrival and departure throughputs and, thus, on-time performance:

- Stochastic issues, which are not under control of airlines and regulators such as weather, mechanical problems, delay propagation
- Demand fluctuations characterized by peak versus non-peak periods, and
- Artificial constraints such as traffic management initiatives.

While considering the aforementioned constraints, ATC, airline and airport operators need to evaluate process capability, that is, the ability of airports to provide 'optimal' arrival and departure capacity to ensure on-time performance. The Z-benchmark describes the six-sigma capability of unutilized airport capacity. The Z-benchmark converts a value in terms of standard deviations from the population mean. It increased from 1.12 (March to May 2015) to 1.37 (March to May 2016) considering the following specifications: a lower limit of 10 percent unutilized airport capacity, a target of 25 percent, and an upper limit of 50 percent. The value of 1.12 and 1.37 measures the number of standard deviations from the center of the distribution to the respective values. In the present case, we define the six-sigma capability as 1.50 + 1.12 = 1.62 in the period from March to May 2015 and 1.50 + 1.37 = 1.87 in the period from March to May 2016. Therefore, the sigma value increased from about 2.6 to 2.9 based on stated specifications. In Figure 2, the opportunities for 'defect' or (Defects per Million Opportunity known as 'DPMO') may refer to delayed gate departure, ramp congestion, late loading of baggage onboard an aircraft, security incident, mismatch between passenger manifest and loaded luggage, taxiway congestion, taxi hold, runway incursion, takeoff queue, among others. In terms of process capability, the percentage of hours between 07:00 and 21:59 that did not meet the specified unutilized airport capacity fell from 13.14 to 8.57 percent.

Pp relates the variation of the distribution to the allowable tolerance specifications. This capability index is a function of the standard deviation and it is different from a nominal (target) value, which may be historical or provided by the customer. The Pp and Ppk represent the long-term capability indexes and they are computed for the whole process without subgrouping (core hours). K stands for 'centralizing factor' to account for the possibility the data may not be centered. The formula for Pp is

$$(USL - LSL) / 6 * \text{standard deviation} \qquad (1).$$

Pp compares the width of the specification to the long-term width of the process. The formula for Ppk is

$$\text{Min} \left[(USL - \mu) / (3 * \text{standard deviation}), (\mu - LSL) / (3 * \text{standard deviation}) \right] \qquad (2),$$

which accounts for the off-centering of the process from the specifications. The Pp and Ppk metrics both indicated an improvement in long-term and adjusted long-term capability (Figure 2).

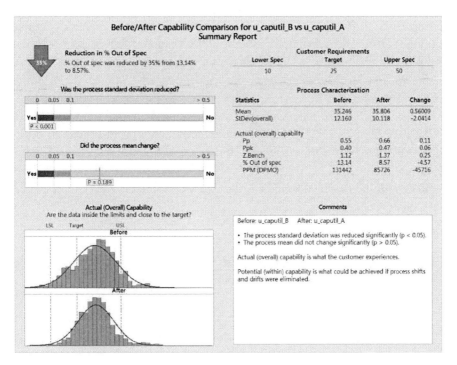

Figure 2. Process Capability Comparison (March-May 2015 as Before and March-May 2016 as After).

DESIGN OF EXPERIMENTS

The design of experiments or DOE represents a significant tool to improve processes. This method allows analysts to test relationship assumptions among variables. It is also a tool to determine cause-and-effect relationships among selected model variables.

The model originally included four factors (total demand, taxi-out time, arrival delay, and airborne delay) that may explain variations in the percentage of unutilized airport capacity. Total demand refers to the sum of arrival and the departure demand. Arrival demand includes the number of aircraft that left the gates at the origin airports and had not yet landed at ATL during an observed hour. Departure demand consists of the aircraft that left the gate at ATL but had not yet taken off during an observed hour. Taxi-out time is the number of minutes it takes for an aircraft to move from gate to takeoff. Arrival delays include the aircraft that arrived at the gate later than the time filed in the flight plan. Airborne delay measures the difference between actual flight time (wheels-off to wheels-on) and estimated time en-route. These variables originate from the Aviation System Performance Metrics (ASPM) data warehouse that contains information on operations and delays. All the variables were measured between the local hours of 07:00 to 21:59, for all days of the week.

The factors were also measured at four levels: minimum value for the 2016 data sample, 25th, 75th, and maximum values. The full factorial design had four factors and four levels, which implied $4^4 = 256$ runs. The α-value for terms to enter and be removed was 0.15. After 256 runs, two variables remained in the final stepwise factorial regression model. The final model can be expressed as follows:

Percentage of unutilized capacity = 84.0 - 0.272*
total demand - 3.53*arrival delay + 0.138* total demand*arrival delay
(3)

The Minitab® output provided the following analysis of variance (ANOVA) tables:

Table 2. Analysis of Variance

Source	DF	Adjusted Sum of Squares	Adjusted Mean Squares	F-Value	P-Value
Model	3	2705.11	901.70	12.08	0.000
Linear	2	597.50	298.75	4.00	0.030
Total Demand	1	177.65	177.65	2.38	0.134
Arrival Delay	1	584.31	584.31	7.83	0.009
2-Way interactions	1	55.72	55.72	0.75	0.395
Total Demand* Arrival Delay	1	55.72	55.72	0.75	0.395
Error	28	2090.29	74.60		

Table 2 indicates that only arrival delay had a significant effect on the unutilized airport capacity. Total demand and the interaction of total demand and arrival delay were not significant at a 95 percent level. Taxi-out times and airborne delays were excluded from the final model.

Although two variables remained after 256 runs, Table 3 indicates that the model explained about 56 percent of the total model variance.

Table 3. Model Summary

Coefficient of Determination (R^2)	R^2 (Adjusted)	R^2 (Predicted)
56.41%	51.74%	40.45%

Table 4 provides the model coefficients. The coefficient for total demand indicates that the mean unutilized capacity decreased by 10.26 percent per one-percent increase in arrival delays, when all other predictors were held constant. Total demand and the interaction of total demand and arrival delay were not significant variables at a 95 percent level. The variance inflation factor or VIF[9] measures how much variance in a factor can be attributed to multicollinearity—when two factors in a model are highly correlated.

Table 4. Model Coefficients

Term	Coefficient	Standard Error Coefficient	T-Value	P-Value	Variance Inflation Factor
Constant	2.02	12.16	0.000		
Total Demand	-10.16	6.59	-1.540	0.134	2.74
Arrival Delay	-10.26	3.67	-2.800	0.009	1.61
Total Demand* Arrival Delay	10.10	11.70	0.860	0.395	3.58

CONCLUSION

This study provides an original perspective on the challenges that air traffic control, airline and airport operators experience in managing of airport capacity. The analysis focused on the variability of unutilized capacity as a key performance indicator of efficient airport capacity management. On-time gate arrivals and departures (on-time performance) represent two metrics that serve to measure efficient capacity management.

---

[9] The formula for VIF is 1 / (1 – R2).

The outcomes of the study imply that airlines cannot meet passengers' expectations of on-time performance if there is not enough available airport capacity to maximize throughputs. On the other hand, too much unutilized capacity may represent a waste of valuable resources. A lean six-sigma approach was used to evaluate and compare the variability of unutilized airport capacity in two samples. A design of experiments enabled to identify the key factors that influenced the percent of unutilized airport capacity.

It is difficult for airlines to collect passengers' requirements and measure their satisfaction. Business travelers are more interested than leisure travelers in services such as seat reservations, baggage leisure travelers are likely to be. They are also more likely to use frequent flier programs, which allows airlines to maintain loyalty and retention. However, this loyalty may quickly erode as an airline cannot ensure on-time connections and overall performance.

This study revealed that on-time performance as the 'voice of the passengers' depended on the variability of unutilized airport capacity and process capability. The analysis started with statistical process control (SPC) to compare the variability of unutilized capacity at ATL between two sampled periods. Second, process capability was used to determine changes in the allocation of airport capacity. Finally, a design of experiments identified arrival delays as a significant factor that may affect the percentage of unutilized airport capacity. Although the mean unutilized airport capacity did not significantly change, the variability of unutilized airport capacity went down from March to May 2016 compared with March to May 2015. An analysis of process capability determined that the sigma improved from about 2.6 (March to May 2015) to 2.9 (March to May 2016) given some parameters.

REFERENCES

Alsyouf, I., Humaid, F., & Al Kamali, S. (2014, December). Mishandled baggage problem: Causes and improvement suggestions. In *2014 IEEE International Conference on Industrial Engineering and Engineering Management*, 154-158.

Ball, M. O., Ausubel, L. M., Berardino, F., Cramton, P., Donohue, G., Hansen, M., & Hoffman, K. (2007). Market-based alternatives for managing congestion at New York's LaGuardia airport. *AirNeth Annual Conference*, The Hague.

Ball, M., Barnhart, C., Dresner, M., Hansen, M., Neels, K., Odoni, A., Peterson, E., Sherry, L., Trani, A., & Zou, B. (October 2010). "Total delay impact study: A comprehensive assessment of the costs and impacts of flight delay in the United States. *The National Center for Excellence for Aviation Operations Research*, http://www.isr.umd.edu/NEXTOR/pubs/TDI_Report_Final_10_18_10_V3.pdf.

Chen, H-L. (2002). Benchmarking and quality improvement: a quality benchmarking deployment approach. *International Journal of Quality & Reliability Management, 19*(6), 757-773.

Chen, F. Y., & Chang, Y. H. (2005). Examining airline service quality from a process perspective. *Journal of Air Transport Management, 11*(2), 79-87.

Cronin, J.J., & Taylor, S.A. (1992). Measuring service quality: a reexamination and extension. *Journal of Marketing, 56*(3), 55-68.

Crosby, P. B. (1980). *Quality is free: The art of making quality certain.* New York: Signet.

Czerny, A. I., & Zhang, A. (2011). Airport congestion pricing and passenger types. *Transportation Research Part B: Methodological, 45*(3), 595-604.

De Neufville, R. (1976). *Airport Systems Planning.* London: Macmillan.

Diana, T. (2015). An evaluation of departure throughputs before and after the implementation of wake vortex recategorization at Atlanta Hartsfield/Jackson International Airport: A Markov regime-switching approach. *Transportation Research Part E: Logistics and Transportation Review, 83*, 216-224.

Gilbert, D., & Wong, R. K. (2003). Passenger expectations and airline services: A Hong Kong based study. *Tourism Management, 24*(5), 519-532.

Goldratt, E. M. (1997). *Critical chain: A business novel.* Great Barrington, MA: North River Press.

Goldratt, E. M. (1990). *Theory of constraints.* Croton-on-Hudson: North River.

Kano, N. (1984). The charming quality and the should-be quality. *Quality Control Journal, 21*(5), 33-41.

Luo, X. (2007). Consumer negative voice and firm-idiosyncratic stock returns. *Journal of Marketing, 71*(3), 75-88.

Pels, E., & Verhoef, E. T. (2004). The economics of airport congestion pricing. *Journal of Urban Economics, 55*(2), 257-277.

Petrick, J. F. (2004). The roles of quality, value, and satisfaction in predicting cruise passengers' behavioral intentions. *Journal of Travel Research, 42*(4), 397-407.

Taguchi, G. (1990) *Introduction to quality engineering: designing quality into products and processes.* Tokyo: Asian Productivity Organization.

U.S. Congress, Office of Technology Assessment (1984). *Airport System Development*, OTA-STI-231.

Wu, C.-L. (2010). Airline operations and delay management: insights from airline economics, networks and strategic schedule planning. Farnham, U.K.: Ashgate.

NOTE

The conclusions of this study do not reflect the official opinion of the Federal Aviation Administration.

BIOGRAPHICAL SKETCH

Tony Diana is the Division Manager, NextGen Performance at the U.S. Federal Aviation Administration. He received his Doctorate in Policy Analysis and Quantitative Management from the University of Maryland Baltimore County. He is involved in the measurement and reporting of operational outcomes resulting from the implementation of NextGen initiatives at U.S. airports, metroplexes and airspaces. Prior to that position, he was Deputy Division Manager, Forecasting and Performance Analysis in the Office of Aviation Policy and Plans of the FAA where he managed the Aviation System Performance Metrics data warehouse. At the Maryland Aviation Administration, he was involved in performance measurement and route development. Dr. Diana's main interests are performance evaluation and benchmarking, as well as the study of delay. Dr. Diana is a Certified Six Sigma Black Belt.

In: Aviation and Airport Security   ISBN: 978-1-53611-909-1
Editor: Don Lawrence   © 2017 Nova Science Publishers, Inc.

Chapter 5

CITIZEN-CENTRIC LINKED DATA APPS FOR EMERGENCY RESPONSE SYSTEMS

Valentina Janev, *Marko Dabović and Sanja Vraneš*

Institute Mihajlo Pupin, University of Belgrade, Serbia

ABSTRACT

One of the most critical aspects of emergency management (EM) is the notification system concerning how to get updated and accurate information from the very first stages of the event and how to notify affected people. The citizens, as the simplest level of participation in an emergency scenario, can act as information consumers (e.g., about alarms, affected areas, instructions for handling critical situation) but also as evidence producers (e.g., via phone or social network).

With the aim to develop a deeper understanding of potential benefits from using Linked Data technologies in emergency scenarios, in this chapter we present our current work on building citizen applications for improved emergency response. The paper introduces first the potential areas of applicability of Linked Data in innovative EM solutions and points to early prototypes in Europe based on crowdsourcing, social networks, mobile devices, and open data. Next, software requirements and information flow are analysed for a data ecosystem that facilitates the engagement of citizens leveraging novel approaches such as the participatory sensing approach (knowledge from the wisdom of crowds) and cloud-enabled solutions.

---

* Email: valentina.janev@institutepupin.com.

To demonstrate the feasibility of the approach, a prototype application, TraffAccs, has been developed using state-of-the-art open-source tools and frameworks: the Massachusetts Institute of Technology (MIT) Panya framework for implementing the mobile client and Dydra graph database for storing notification messages.

Keywords: linked data, traffic accident, citizen engagement, mobile apps, emergency notification

INTRODUCTION

Emergency management (EM) is a complex field, with a lot of different active and passive stakeholders that need to perform complex tasks in a short time. EM generally has four aspects: preparedness, response, mitigation, and recovery. The main goals of EM systems (EMS) in the response and mitigation phases are detection, evaluation, and confirmation of alarms; determination of the location and extent of an incident; and provision of automated reaction and/or assistance and decision support to the first responders and EM personnel. The emergency notification system, concerning how to get updated and accurate information from the very first stages of the event and how to notify affected people [1], is one of the most critical aspects of the response phase.

Recent information technology developments have influenced the evolution of e-government services, and in particular the emergency services. The shift from analog to internet protocol (IP) surveillance cameras, for instance, has changed the way that video surveillance systems are built [2]. In Europe, 112 is the common emergency telephone number that can be dialed free of charge to reach emergency services (ambulance, fire and rescue, police) through the public switched telephone or mobile networks. Voice over internet protocol (VoIP) devices and applications have become commonplace. However, with the rise of new technologies and applications, all citizens everywhere in the world expect to be able to contact emergency services with technologies they use to communicate every day, including mobile devices and social websites. For instance, a 2009 study [3] commissioned by the American Red Cross found that social media sites are the fourth most popular source to access emergency information. Social media sites have been used by individuals and communities to warn others of unsafe areas or situations, inform friends and family that someone is safe, and raise funds for disaster relief. A good example is the tsunami disaster in Japan in 2011. During this event the authorities realized that a big amount of updated information was broadcast via Twitter, revealing the public usefulness and effectiveness of social networks [4]. For an updated list of mobile applications used for emergency notification we refer to the work of Romano et al. [1].

In the last decade, European Union (EU) and national governments allocated funds to innovate emergency services and promote research in the EM area. The European Standard eCall that will be mandatory in 2018 is designed to use standard Global System for Mobile (GSM) communications voice channels. eCall is an in-vehicle road safety system which automatically calls the emergency services in case of a serious accident, even if the driver and passengers are unconscious (see Figure 1). It is expected that the emergency (112) calls will be routed by the mobile network operator to the most appropriate public safety answering points (PSAP), which are dependent on the origin of the emergency call and the nature of the call. This origin is a geographical area identified by the official municipal identifier for emergency calls. In case of a crash, an eCall-equipped car automatically calls the network service provider. Even if no passenger is able to speak, e.g., due to injuries, a minimum set of data (MSD) is sent, which includes the exact location of the crash site, direction of travel, and vehicle description.

In addition to this initiative, some countries are in a process of adoption of additional notification services. For instance in Spain the SafetyGPS application is a Twitter-based platform developed for sending tweets to a list of local city halls [1].

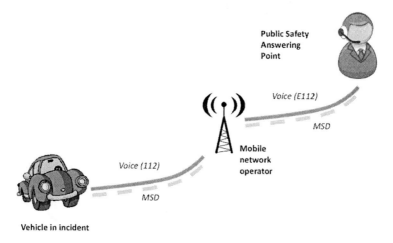

Figure 1. European eCall conceptual model.

This chapter aims at obtaining a deeper understanding of potential benefits from using innovative approaches, in particular the Linked Data paradigm, in scenarios related to traffic accidents. The work builds upon and extends previous efforts [5]. The overall goal is to explore their role in building interoperable safety and security city infrastructures (as part of the national EM infrastructure) and transforming the way citizen-centric safe smart city services are delivered.

The chapter is organized as follows: First highlighted are recent research studies and recently developed prototypes that leverage Linked Data technologies and social media to enhance situation awareness. Then we analyze the potential role of citizens in emergency response actions and point to the need of establishing a bidirectional channel between EM operators and citizens for improved EM. Software infrastructure for facilitating the engagement of citizens is presented next, followed by proof of concept (prototype application TraffAccs).

RELATED WORK

Linked Open Data

In the last few years the Linked Data paradigm has evolved as a powerful enabler for the transition of the current document-oriented web into a web of interlinked data and, ultimately, into the semantic web. The term Linked Data here refers to a set of best practices for publishing and connecting structured data on the web. These best practices have been adopted by an increasing number of data providers over the past five years, leading to the creation of a global data space that contains many billions of assertions, the Linked Open Data (LOD) cloud [6]. Although in the past, governments were protective of the data they collected, citing national security and citizen privacy, recently they (especially the U.S. and the U.K.) have participated actively in the Open Government Data initiative. The Open Government Data initiative aims at motivating governments and organizations to make information freely available and easily accessible online. The benefits of Open Government Data are economic, through the identification of new business opportunities, and social, through increased transparency, participation, and accountability.

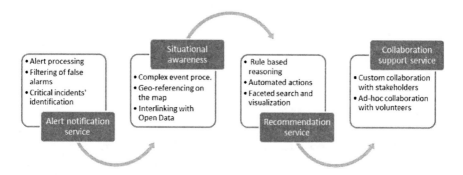

Figure 2. Main functionalities in EMS.

Linked Data Technologies and EM Systems

Studying the possibilities of using Linked Data technologies to improve the main functionalities of EMS [5], we have identified four application areas, namely: alert notification, situational awareness, action execution and recommendation, and collaboration (see Figure 2). These were the study's conclusions:

- Messages typically exchanged during incidents/disasters can be modelled by reusing established vocabularies and creating new ones when necessary to ease semantic interpretation of data from different sources; see, for example, recommended standards (EDXL).
- *Data Extraction* and *Transformation*, as well as *Enrichment* and *Interlinking* can be used to make more data available, eventually resulting in improved situational awareness (through visualization of the new data) and better recommendations given by the system (through processing of the new data), as more information would be available.
- *Crowdsourced information* can include more people in EM, thus contributing to collaboration and situational awareness and posing an additional source of alerts.

Related Work

For several years the Fire department of the Netherlands has been investing business intelligence approaches for improved accident prevention and accident fighting. LOD were used as a business intelligence approach for the creation of dwelling fire risk profiles based on demographic data [7]. The Fire Department Amsterdam-Amstelland used Linked Data principles for real-time publication of incident data through the Kasabi platform [8].

In a theoretical elaboration of the use of LOD in EM, Borges et al. [9] proposed a scheme for collecting available data from government agencies, such as departments of health, transport, works, that can supply information needed during an emergency response operation. In addition to standard software architecture composed of data, integration, application, and user layer, the proposed Collaborative Knowledge Management Architecture includes Linked Data processing and semantic layer.

Schulz et al. [10] leverage LOD and crowdsourcing for processing data from social media and show how the combination of human intelligence in the crowd and automatic approaches for enhancing the situational picture with LOD will lead to a Web 3.0 approach for more efficient information handling in crisis management.

Terpstra et al. [11] investigated the possibilities of real-time and automated analysis of Twitter messages during crises. Automated analysis was performed through application of the information extraction tool Twitcident, a working prototype that so far has not been applied for real-time information extraction purposes.

Thus it was recognized that LOD offered a high potential to improve information integration, situational awareness, and collaboration during disaster and emergency response [12]. Furthermore, LOD could revolutionize information gathering and decision support. However, challenges related to real-time processing of linked data should be properly addressed.

Problem Statement

Community engagement is a growing practice in management of urban issues. It is defined as "the process of enabling participation of citizens and communities in policing at their chosen level, ranging from providing information and reassurance, to empowering them to identify and implement solutions to local problems and influence strategic priorities and decisions" [13]. In an emergency situation, citizens directly involved as victims or witnesses, e.g., in a traffic accident (see Figure 3), and thus being aware of updated information useful for managing the situation, can play an important role in first response activities [1].

Using an emergency notification service, witnesses could easily create alerts and share information about the traffic accident (e.g., affected areas, what, when, where, number of injured) with law enforcement officials. Instead of using a *one-way channel* that transmits emergency messages to a specific receiver or a group of people, a *bidirectional channel* could be established between EM operators and citizens for receiving and sending information in real time through an emergency communication system [14]. Besides being producers of evidence, in an emergency communication system, citizens are consumers of information, e.g., instructions for handling a critical situation or instructions to avoid critical places. A very simplified flow of information between the main actors can be summarized as following:

[*event at T1*]: A traffic accident happens at a crossroad with great material damage and few injured.
[*event at T2*]: Person A, a witness of the incident reports via a *participatory* information service (two-way service between the citizen and the city).
[*action at T3*]: Traffic congestion and accidents web service is updated.
[*action at T4*]: Previous events will trigger actions such as a police officer appears on the scene, a first aid car arrives, and social media harvesting is started to build archives for state bodies entitled to resolve the accident.
[*event at T5*]: Person B, located at a certain distance, receives information on the event and has the ability to choose an alternative travel route to avoid creating long lines of vehicles and thus a traffic jam.

Figure 3. Traffic accident (Niš, Serbia, http://niskevesti.rs, 25.11.2016).

This simplified flow of information suggests that interoperable communication and security networks and systems are needed that allow emergency operators and stakeholders (citizens, first responders, mobile operators) to share the same databases, to collect and reconcile information in order to detect events or incidents, and to deploy the right resources to deal with the situation. Such systems will collect and correlate events from various existing security systems and security devices (video, access control, sensors, analytics, networks, etc.) to help official personnel to solve situations.

Research focus: Our aim in this research is thus to (1) identify the main characteristics of citizen-centric participatory sensing tools, (2) design and prototype emergency notification applications, and (3) study the limitations that could be relevant for introducing innovations in the current practice of reporting traffic accidents and sending notifications and information to public authorities. The analysis focuses mainly on bringing to light the kind of interaction, the functionalities, the content that can be shared and the recipients of the messages.

Related to technologies needed to innovate in current traffic accident EM practices, our research focus will be on using the Linked Data paradigm, databases and semantic technologies, open source tools, and cloud platforms such as the Dydra platform for prototyping the solution.

SOFTWARE INFRASTRUCTURE FOR FACILITATING CITIZEN ENGAGEMENT

In this section we will introduce our vision for an innovative and smart emergency communication system incorporating the following advantages:

- Leverage recent technological advances (stream processing, Linked Data technologies) and available sensing mechanisms (on mobile devises) to collect insightful information and generate actionable information, thus making a city more transparent and responsive.
- Empower citizens in smart cities to participate in emergency prevention and management (crowdsourcing) by ensuring that the main urban dynamics are unveiled and available to the public.
- Allow citizens to share information and experiences in real-time streaming and to receive alerts and messages from security command and control centers.

- Close the information gap between security personnel, law enforcement agencies (LEAs), and citizens by establishing dedicated input and output communication channels for coordination and joint efforts.

Cities' Data Ecosystem for Emergency Response

Today the internet is widely used for globally communicating and disseminating information. As a result of enormous work done by national governments around the Open Data initiative, and volunteering efforts such as DBpedia,[1] Open Street Map,[2] and LinkedGeoData,[3] there is a limitless amount of available online resources and tools to share information and develop a better understanding on whatever topics. In Figure 4 a data ecosystem is proposed that is intrinsically complex, as it has numerous stakeholders with differing goals and needs. Taking into consideration that government agencies worldwide [15] have recognized the potential of social networks in the EM process—and in particular for situation awareness and notification in crisis situation—we propose an approach that foresees the modern mobile phones and social networks (such as Twitter) as commonly used channels for raising awareness about events. The guiding idea for this approach was the need to create a software solution that will allow users (witnesses) to very easily create information about a traffic accident and share the evidence via channels dedicated for that purpose without extensive knowledge of police or other procedures. The integrated vision of the software solution is presented in Figure 4.

Data Producer Side: When a traffic accident occurs, citizens represented as data producers in Figure 4 will use a mobile application, TraffAccs, to exchange real-time information with operations centers involved in response activities. The goal is to support the first and perhaps the most important phase when witnesses need to collect information about the situation and notify the law enforcement agency and the wider community. This data is stored on the server side, can be used in real time as evidence, as well as later for a variety of analyses carried out by state institutions and/or insurance companies. TraffAccs ensures that the evidence is geocoded and as such, can be easily

---

[1] http://wiki.dbpedia.org/.
[2] http://www.openstreetmap.org/.
[3] http://www.linkedgeodata.org/.

interlinked and enriched with other open data, for instance, the closest police patrol that can be assigned and can be entitled to resolve the situation.

Data Consumer Side: Two implementation strategies have been considered for notifying citizens in an emergency. People who use the TraffAccs application for smart mobile devices, if close to the accident location, could be informed about the event by services that run on the server side (see Figure 4, Case I). The prerequisite for proper functioning of the TraffAccs application is that the user has allowed other devices to collect his or her current location (GPS notification). Public authorities, who have access to the entire database, will be able to design and build analytical services so they respond to the situation in a timely manner. An alternative to the first case is to integrate into TraffAccs a service that will regularly exchange information with the server and check for threats (see Figure 4, Case II).

Software Requirements

Putting in place a citizen-centric sensing application to help collect data and evidence on traffic accidents via social media and to store the data in one place requires on one side an effort to develop citizen-centric sensing applications and on the other an effort to adapt information systems used by the emergency agencies to the channels that people are already used to (e.g., Twitter or Facebook).

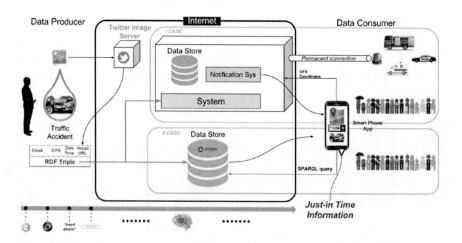

Figure 4. Information flow in proposed solution system.

On the data producer's side, the citizen-centric sensing application might provide possibilities such as these:

- Sending victim requests for assistance.
- Sending evidence and uploading images to be available for damage estimates, among others.
- Compiling lists of the dead and injured, and sending information to victims' friends and family members.

On the data consumer's side, software infrastructure (that includes the citizen-centric sensing application and the cloud-based emergency communication system) might provide these functions;

- Monitoring user activities and postings to establish situational awareness.
- Conducting emergency communications and issuing warnings.
- Sending instructions for more efficient dealing with the emerging situation (for those ill prepared for an incident).
- Alerting citizens and first responders to changing conditions and new threats.

PROOF OF CONCEPT: PROTOTYPE APPLICATION TRAFFACCS

Using TraffAccs

The TraffAccs application was developed to test feasibility especially in the domain of innovative technologies such as cloud platforms, Linked Data paradigm, and graph processing, mobile devices. The application is based on the Android operating system. After starting the application, the user logs in to his or her Twitter account (see Figure 5) and then takes a picture of the incident using the camera and enters details of the accident (type of accident, e.g., with death, injuries, material damage) (see Figure 4). The date and time of the accident is created automatically when the user takes the photo. By pressing the 'submit' button, the data will be stored on the Dydra server in RDF triple form (see Figure 4). The application will inform the user about uploading of information in the data store.

Table 1. Components used to build the TraffAccs application

Palette	Description[4]
Nonvisible components	
Camera	Media component takes a picture using the device's camera. After the picture is taken, the name of the file on the phone containing the picture is available as an argument to the *AfterPicture* event.
Location sensor	Sensor component providing location information, including longitude, latitude, altitude (if supported by the device), and address. This can also perform geocoding, converting an address (not necessarily the current one) to a latitude (with the *LatitudeFromAddress* method) and a longitude (with the *LongitudeFromAddress* method). Location sensor should be enabled (property *Enabled* set to *True*), and the device should allow location sensing through wireless networks or GPS satellites (if outdoors). Location information might not be available immediately when an app starts. The user will have to wait a short time for a location provider to be found and used or wait for the *OnLocationChanged* event.
LinkedData	Linked Data component.
Twitter	Social component that enables communication with Twitter. Once a user has logged into their Twitter account (and the authorization has been confirmed as successful by the *Is Authorized* event), many more operations are available: • Searching Twitter for tweets or labels (*SearchTwitter*) • Sending a Tweet (*Tweet*) • Sending a Tweet with an Image (*TweetWithImage*) • Directing a message to a specific user (*DirectMessage*) • Receiving the most recent messages directed to the logged-in user (*RequestDirectMessages*) • Following a specific user (*Follow*) • Ceasing to follow a specific user (*StopFollowing*) • Getting a list of users following the logged-in user (*RequestFollowers*) • Getting the most recent messages of users followed by the logged-in user (*RequestFriendTimeline*) • Getting the most recent mentions of the logged-in user (*RequestMentions*)
Palette	Description
Clock	Sensor component that provides the instant in time using the internal clock on the phone. It can fire a timer at regularly set intervals and perform time calculations, manipulations, and conversions. Methods to convert an instant to text are also available. Acceptable patterns

[4] Descriptions taken from http://punya.appinventor.mit.edu/reference/components.

Palette	Description
Clock	are empty string, MM/DD/YYYY HH:mm:ss a, or MMM d, yyyy HH:mm. The empty string will provide the default format, which is "MMM d, yyyy HH:mm:ss a" for FormatDateTime and "MMM d, yyyy" for FormatDate.
Visible components – User Interface (UI)	
Button	Buttons are components that users touch to perform some action in the app. Buttons detect when users tap them. Many aspects of a button's appearance can be changed. You can use the Enabled property to choose whether a button can be tapped. In TraffAccs the following buttons are used: *Twitter, Camera, Submit,* and *Location.*
TextBox	Users enter text in a text box component. The initial or user-entered text value in a text box component is in the Text property. If *Text* is blank, you can use the *Hint* property to provide the user with a suggestion of what to type. The *Hint* appears as faint text in the box. In TraffAccs, *TextBox* is used for inserting details.
Label	Labels are components used to show text. A label displays text specified by the Text property. Other properties, all of which can be set in the Designer or Blocks Editor, control the appearance and placement of the text. In TraffAccs are labels for presenting date and time, location and caption.
LinkedData-Form	A form for grouping data properties. LinkedDataForm is subject, grouped data are predicates, and their data are objects in RDF tripe. In TraffAccs, *LineddDataForm* is used (see Figure 7).

Punya Framework and the Design of TraffAccs

The TraffAccs application for smart mobile devices was designed and developed using the Punya framework, derivative of the Massachusetts Institute of Technology (MIT) App Inventor platform for developing Android applications. Programming is block based, meaning that application development is very fast, which helps researchers focus on solving the problem. The Punya framework provides easy access to sensors and other personal information on the smartphone. For example, the Punya framework has sensor components for reading the GPS location, taking photos with the camera, receiving SMS texts, and sending Twitter messages.

Figure 5. Using TraffAccs.

Figure 6. Visual programming language in Punya framework.

Dydra Cloud-Based Graph Database

For realization of the second scenario illustrated in Figure 4, Dydra[5], a powerful graph database in the cloud was used (see Figure 6). Dydra was designed as a semantic data management tool by experts at MIT's Computer Science and Artificial Intelligence Laboratory (CSAIL)[6] with the aim to provide a quick and easy way to develop Android applications based on Linked Data principles. In case of a traffic accident the user describes the accident in the Text Box on the TraffAccs GUI (see object *TypeOfAccident* in Figure 7) and specifies a link to the image stored on the Twitter server (object *Image*). The *DataTime* and the *Location* object are created automatically. The RDF triples stored on the cloud server comprise the alert message that should trigger additional actions by public authorities.

---

[5] Retrieved February 22, 2017, from https://dydra.com/.
[6] Retrieved February 22, 2017, from http://www.csail.mit.edu/.

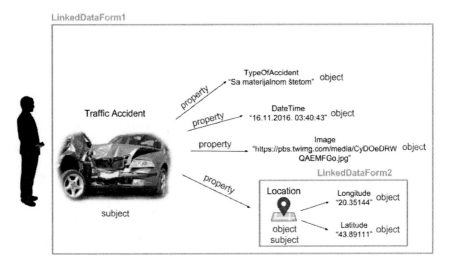

Figure 7. Example of grouping properties and creating RDF triples.

CONCLUSIONS

Smart technologies revolutionize the way the cities locate, mitigate, and prevent safety issues. The current prototype demonstrates the use of the TraffAccs application in the data collection process only. Although in this very early phase it is obvious that the solution has advantages over the classical traffic accident notification channels because it provides means to collect a lot of information in a very simple and efficient way (plenty of precise and accurate information important for the accident situation). However the adoption of the application should be analyzed in the wider EU context.

Fostering Semantic Interoperability at EU Level

Since 1995 the European Commission has conducted several interoperability solutions programs, in which the last one shall be active during the next five years (2016-2020) under the name Interoperability Solutions for European Public Administrations (ISA)[2] (http://ec.europa.eu/isa/isa2/). The holistic approach (G2G, G2C, G2B) foresees four levels of interoperability, namely, legal, organizational, semantic, and technical (syntactical) interoperability. In the domain of emergency services implementation, EU member states are quite independent, meaning that each stakeholder has deployed its own system of command, control, and communication. As a direct result of this situation, EMSs and information data models and formats are invariably incompatible with each other, meaning that cooperation between emergency forces becomes almost impossible in many regions [16]. Moreover, in an international European context, the situation with regard to the EMS-to-EMS information exchange provides a number of challenges, considering not only technical interoperability, but also diversity in language and cultural particularities, legal issues (different regulation, complex legal landscape), or data representation (inconsistent color codes, different graphical symbol sets), among others.

Hence, in order to ensure wider adoption of the prototype application TraffAccs (Section 5), first on the country and then on the EU level, the syntactical (ability of TraffAccs to communicate and exchange information properly) and semantical (ability to automatically interpret the information exchanged meaningfully and accurately) issues should be addressed first.

Facilitating Information Sharing and Integration of Collected Evidence with Existing EMS

In order to support citizen participation, i.e., sharing data via social media, Twitter, and smartphone apps, as well as receiving alerts and messages from security command and control centers, special interface services should be built that could be implemented as cloud services, as illustrated in Figure 4.

Therefore, our future work in this context will be to elaborate the *software infrastructure for facilitating the engagement of citizens* in more details and define the vocabularies, taxonomies, classifications, and thesauri that will be used for message exchange. This communication can take place either by standards [17] or by message mapping to convert the data. In TraffAccs, the intention is to base implementation on conceptual approaches refined in recent EU projects such as Reliable and Smart Crowdsourcing Solution for Emergency and Crisis Management (RESCUER) (http://www.rescuer-project.org/), Data Interoperability Solution at Stakeholders Emergency Reaction (DISASTER) (http://disaster-fp7.eu/), [18] and Seamless Communication for Crisis Management (SECRICOM) (http://www.secricom.eu/) projects, as well as on European Emergency Number Association (EENA) recommendations [19].

Improving Situational Awareness with Open Data

Situational awareness on the producers or consumers side (see Figure 4) could be improved first by annotating and then interlinking the important keywords from alert messages or reports on the situation with other open resources such as DBpedia and Open Street Maps. Therefore, as part of future work we will study the possibility of integrating TraffAccs with mobile geospatial visualization and exploration tools such as the Mobile Semantic Geospatial Visualization and Exploration tool [20] that supports faceted browsing over RDF datasets on handheld devices. Faceted browsing builds upon faceted classification, an analytic-synthetic classification scheme which uses multiple taxonomies to classify objects [21]. Thus, information available in Open Data format can be loaded and filtered according to the user's needs, e.g., the closest police stations, as well as the nearest health centers. Further on, the tool leverages smartphone capabilities to deliver semantic routing based on open, crowd-sourced, and semantically linked information found in publicly available sources, such as the LOD Cloud.[7] The feature is immensely useful for users on the go, especially when they find themselves in an unknown or changed environment (e.g., roads are blocked due to an accident).

Applicability of the Approach in Airport Security Scenarios

Airports are some of the most complex and demanding critical infrastructures, representing the critical hub for air transportation of people and goods. Emergency situations that occur at airports are divided into aircraft emergencies and terminal and ground emergencies. The approach discussed in this chapter can be used in the context of a car accident in the area surrounding the airport and/or on airport access roads. In case the traffic accident is close to the airport building, usually the situation will be resolved by airport emergency personnel in accordance with existing procedures for ground emergencies. However, if massive and multidomain data need to be processed quickly in airport EMS, cloud computing (see Figure 4) may be adopted to design more satisfactory systems with higher processing speed, larger storage memory, less risk, lower cost, and higher capability for integration [22].

---

[7] Retrieved February 22, 2017, http://lod-cloud.net/.

ACKNOWLEDGMENTS

The research presented in this paper is financed by the Ministry of Science and Technological Development of the Republic of Serbia (SOFIA project, Pr. No: TR-32010).

REFERENCES

[1] Romano, M., Onorati, T., Aedo, I., Diaz, P. (2016). Designing mobile applications for emergency response: Citizens acting as human sensors. *Sensors 16*(3), 406.

[2] Top 14 best practices for building video surveillance networks. http://smartcitiescouncil.com/resources/top-14-best-practices-building-video-surveillance-networks.

[3] The American Red Cross (2009). Web users increasingly rely on social media to seek help in a disaster. Washington, DC: ARC.

[4] Ichiguchi, T. (2011). Robust and Usable Media for Communication in a Disaster. *Quarterly Review* 4, 44-55. http://data.nistep.go.jp/dspace/bitstream/11035/2871/1/NISTEP-STT041E-44.pdf.

[5] Mijović, V., Janev, V., Vraneš, S. (2013). Main challenges in using LOD in emergency management scenarios. In: Proceedings of the 3rd International Workshop on Information Systems for Situation Awareness and Situation Management. ISSASiM '13 in conjunction with the 24th International Conference on Database and Expert Systems Applications (DEXA), Prague, Czech Republic. Danvers, MA: IEEE Computer Society, 21-25

[6] Auer, S., Lehmann, J. (2010). Making the web a data washing machine: Creating knowledge out of interlinked data. *Semantic Web Journal* 1(12), 97-104.

[7] van Oorschot, N., van Leeuwen, B. (2015). Intelligent fire risk monitor based on Linked Open Data. SHARE-PSI Workshop, Berlin, 2017. https://www.w3.org/2013/share-psi/wiki/images/9/9b/Thesis_V1_Presentations_Paper_-_Intelligent_fire_risk_monitor_based_on_Linked_Open_Data.pdf.

[8] van Leeuwen, B. (2012). Real-time emergency response using semantic web technology. Semantic Technology & Business Conference, Berlin.

http://semtechbizberlin2012.semanticweb.com/sessionPop.cfm?confid=6
6&proposalid=4431.

[9]   Borges, M. R. S., de Faria Cordeiro, K., Campos, M. L. M., Marino, T.
       (2011). Linked open data and the design of information infrastructure for
       emergency management systems. In: M. A. Santos, L. Sousa, E. Portela
       (eds). Proceedings of the 8th International Conference on Information
       Systems for Crisis Response and Management. Lisbon, Portugal.

[10]   Schulz, A., Paulheim, H., Probst, F. (2012). Crisis information
       management in the web 3.0 age. Proceedings of the 9th International
       ISCRAM Conference. Vancouver, Canada. http://www.iscramlive.
       org/ISCRAM2012/proceedings/160.pdf.

[11]   Terpstra, T., de Vries, A., Stronkman, R., Paradies, G. L. (2012).
       Towards a real-time Twitter analysis during crises for operational crisis
       management. Proceedings of the 9th International Conference on
       Information Systems for Crisis Response and Management, Vancouver,
       Canada.

[12]   Ortman, J., Limbu, M., Wang, D., Kauppinen T. (2011). Crowdsourcing
       linked open data for disaster management. Proceedings of the 9th
       International Conference on Information Systems for Crisis Response
       and Management, Bonn, Germany.

[13]   Myhill, A. (2006). Community engagement in policing: Lessons from
       the literature. London: Home Office. http://college.police.uk/en/docs/
       Community_engagement_lessons.pdf.

[14]   Poole, J. (2015). Understanding emergency communication systems, risk
       analysis, and voice intelligibility. PE, FSFPE. https://energy.gov/
       sites/prod/files/2015/06/f22/10-Poole-Understanding-ECS-Risk%
       20Analysis-and-Voice-Intelligibility.pdf.

[15]   Lindsay, B. R. (2011). Social media and disasters: Current uses, future
       options, and policy considerations. Congressional Research Service.
       https://www.files.ethz.ch/isn/133049/R41987.pdf.

[16]   Schütte, F., Casado, R., Rubiera, E. (2013). Solving interoperability
       issues in cross border emergency operations. In: T. Comes, F. Fiedrich,
       S. Fortier, J. Geldermann, T. Müller (eds). Proceedings of the 10th
       International Conference on Information Systems for Crisis Response
       and Management, Baden-Baden, Germany.

[17]   Barros, R., Kislansky, P., Salvador, L., Almeida, R., Breyer, M.,
       Pedraza, L. G., Vieira, V. (2015). EDXL-RESCUER ontology: An
       update based on faceted taxonomy approach. Journal of Medical
       Systems 2015.

[18] Casado, R., Rubiera, E., Sacristan, M., Schütte, F. Peters, R. (2015). Data interoperability software solution for emergency reaction in the Europe Union. *Nat. Hazards Earth Syst. Sci.* 15, 1563–1576.

[19] Data sharing between emergency services (2015). EENA operations document. http://www.eena.org/download.asp?item_id=151.

[20] Milošević, U., Stadler, C. (2015). Mobile semantic geospatial visualization and exploration. In: M. Zdravković, M. Trajanović, Z. Konjović (eds). Proceedings of the International Conference on Information Society and Techology. 160-164.

[21] Gödert, W. (1991). Facet classification in online retrieval. *International Classification* 18(2), 98-109.

[22] Gelenbe, E., Wu, F. (2013). Future research on cyber-physical emergency management systems. *Future Internet* 5, 336-354.

Reviewed by Dr. Mladen Stanojević, School of Computing, University Union, Belgrade (http://raf.edu.rs/en/about-us1/teachers-and-associates)

AUTHOR BIOGRAPHICAL SKETCHES

Valentina Janev

Affiliation: Institute Mihajlo Pupin, University of Belgrade, Serbia

Education: Graduated in Electrical Engineering and received her master's degree in Computer Science from the University of Ljubljana, Slovenia. She received her PhD degree in Semantic Web Technologies from the University of Belgrade, School of Electrical Engineering and Computer Science.

Business Address: Volgina 15, 11060 Belgrade, Serbia

Research and Professional Experience: She has participated in design and implementation of many information systems including government applications. Since 2003 she is involved in scientific projects financed by the Serbian Ministry of Science, as well as in EU FP6, FP7, and HORIZON 2020 projects. These include SlideWiki, large-scale pilots for collaborative OpenCourseware authoring, multiplatform delivery, and learning analytics; Web4WeB, Web technologies for West Balkan countries; Emergency Management in Large Infrastructures (EMILI); LOD2, Creating Knowledge out of Interlinked Data; GeoKnow, making the web an exploratory place for geospatial data; Higher Education Leading to Engineering and Scientific

Careers (HELENA); GenderTime, Transferring Implementing Monitoring Equality; and Platform for Trans-Academic Cooperation in Innovation (PACINNO). Her interests include semantic web, applications of semantic technologies, W3C standards in knowledge management, knowledge management architectures for R&D organizations, e-government, and emergency services. She has published a book and around 80 papers as journal, book, conference, and workshop contributions in these fields. She serves as reviewer for international journals including *International Journal on Semantic Web and Information Systems* (IGI Global), *International Journal of Digital Earth* (Taylor & Francis), *Information Systems Management* (Taylor & Francis), *International Journal of Intelligent Information Systems* (Science Publishing Group), and *American Journal of Software Engineering and Applications* (Science Publishing Group).

Professional Appointments: Valentina Janev is senior researcher at the Institute Mihajlo Pupin, University of Belgrade, Serbia.

Marko M. Dabović,
MSc, PhD, student of Computer Science

Affiliation: School of Electrical Engineering, University of Belgrade, Serbia

Education: Graduated in Computer Science from the School of Electrical Engineering, University of Belgrade, Serbia

Business Address: Bulevar kralja Aleksandra 73, 11120 Belgrade, Serbia

Research and Professional Experience: He is experienced in software design and development, web application architecture, client/server programming, data modeling, user interface design, database, mobile applications, and game development. He has expert knowledge of numerous programming languages and technologies, including Java, C#, C++, and JavaScript. His interests include programming languages, CUDA parallelization, mobile development, artificial intelligence—deep learning, the application of information technology in the field of medical sciences, web technology design and implementation. His focus is the design, analysis, and implementation of software systems. He has worked on student projects in the area of robotics (e.g., simulation of the movement of the robot arm with 5 DOF, designing systems for manipulation of the robot arm via internet) and augmented reality (AR) Android apps which are used in various domains. He holds a PhD scholarship from the Ministry of Education, Science and Technological Development of the Republic of Serbia.

Sanja Vraneš, PhD

Affiliation: Institute Mihajlo Pupin, University of Belgrade, Serbia

Education: Graduated in Electrical Engineering and received her PhD degree from the University of Belgrade, School of Electrical Engineering and Computer Science.

Business Address: Volgina 15, 11060 Belgrade, Serbia

Research and Professional Experience: Since 1999 she has been engaged as a UN expert in information technologies and since 2005 as expert evaluator and reviewer of EC Framework Program Projects and H2020 projects. Her research interests include semantic web, linked data web, knowledge management, decision support systems. She has published over 200 scientific papers. She serves as a reviewer of international journals including *IEEE Transaction on Computer* and *IEEE Intelligent Systems* magazine. She was a postdoctoral research fellow at the University of Bristol, U.K., in 1993 and 1994. In 1999-2004 she was scientific consultant at the ICS-UNIDO, International Center for Science and High Technology in Trieste, Italy. She has served as project leader and/or principal architect for more than 20 commercial software projects. She is a member of IEEE, ACM, and AAAI. She is a member of the Serbian Academy of Engineering Sciences and of the National Scientific Council.

Professional Appointments: Sanja Vraneš, PhD, is jointly appointed as director general of the Mihajlo Pupin Institute and as full professor of Computer Science at the University of Belgrade.

Publications from the Last Three Years

1.   Janev, V., Paunović, D., Jovanović-Vasović, J., Orčević, S., Vraneš, S. (2016). Chapter 8: Serbia. In: C. Cozza, G. Harirchi, A. Marković Čunko (eds). *Innovation in the Adriatic Region*. EUT Edicioni Universita di Trieste. ISBN 978-88-8303-761-0 (762-7 Online).
2.   Janev, V., Vraneš, S. (2015). Semantic web. In: P. A. Laplante (ed). *Encyclopedia of Information Systems and Technology*. Taylor & Francis.
3.   Van Nuffelen, B., Janev, V., Martin, M., Mijovic, V., Tramp, S. (2014). Supporting the linked data life cycle using an integrated tool stack. In: S. Auer, V. Bryl, S. Tramp (eds). *Linked Open Data: Creating Knowledge Out of Interlinked Data*. Lecture Notes in Computer Science vol. 8661, pp. 108–129. Springer International Publishing. ISBN 978-3-319-09845-6 (Print); 978-3-319-09846-3 (Online).

4. Van der Waal, S., Węcel, K., Ermilov, I., Janev, V., Milošević, U., Wainwright, M. (2014). Lifting open data portals to the data web. In: S. Auer, V. Bryl, S. Tramp (eds). *Linked Open Data: Creating Knowledge Out of Interlinked Data*. Lecture Notes in Computer Science vol. 8661, pp. 175–195. Springer International Publishing. ISBN 978-3-319-09845-6 (Print); 978-3-319-09846-3 (Online).

5. Mijović, V. Janev, V., Paunović, D., Vraneš, S. (2016) Exploratory spatio-temporal analysis of linked statistical data. *Journal of Web Semantics*. Web Semantics: Science, Services and Agents on the World Wide Web. 41C, pp. 1-8.

6. Lackshen, G., Vraneš, S., Janev, V. (2016). Big data and quality: A literature review. In: Proceedings of 24th Telecommunications Forum (TELFOR), Belgrade, Serbia. ISBN 978-1-5090-4085-8. http://ieeexplore.ieee.org/document/7818902/.

7. Janev, V., Mijović, V., Vraneš, S. (2016). Proposal for implementing the EU PSI directive in Serbia. In: A. Kő, E. Francesconi. Proceedings of the Fifth International Conference on Electronic Government and the Information Systems Perspective (EGOVIS), Porto, Portugal. Lecture Notes in Computer Science, pp 16-30. Springer International Publishing. http://link.springer.com/chapter/10.1007%2F978-3-319-44159-7_2.

8. Janev, V., Mijović, V., Vraneš, S. (2016). Statistical metadata management in European eGovernment systems. In: M. Zdravković, M. Trajanović, Z. Konjović (eds). Proceedings of the Sixth International Conference on Information Society Technology, Kopaonik, Serbia. Society for Information Systems and Computer Networks.

9. Mijović, V., Janev, V., Paunović, D. (2016). Transformation and analysis of spatio-temporal statistical linked open data with ESTA-LD. In: M. Zdravković, M. Trajanović, Z. Konjović (eds). Proceedings of the Sixth International Conference on Information Society Technology, Kopaonik, Serbia. Society for Information Systems and Computer Networks.

10. Mijović, V., Janev, V., Paunović, D. (2015). ESTA-LD: Enabling spatio-temporal analysis of linked statistical data. In: M. Zdravković, M. Trajanović, Z. Konjović (eds) Proceedings of the Fifth International Conference on Information Society Technology, Kopaonik, Serbia. Society for Information Systems and Computer Networks. http://www.yuinfo.org/icist2015/Proceedings_ICIST_2015.pdf.

11. Janev, V., Mijović, V., Paunović, D., Milošević, U. (2014). Modeling, fusion and exploration of regional statistics and indicators with linked data tools. In: A. Kő, E. Francesconi (eds). Electronic Government and

the Information Systems Perspective. Proceedings of the Third International Conference (EGOVIS), Munich, Germany. Lecture Notes in Computer Science vol. 8650, pp. 208-221. Springer International Publishing. ISBN 978-3-319-10177-4 (Print); 978-3-319-10178-1 (Online); Series ISSN 0302-9743.

INDEX